Looking

for

VIDETUR
MIHI
UTI
PALEA

F.E.Sparshott

Philosophy

McGill-Queens
University Press
Montreal and London 1972

© 1972 McGill-Queen's University Press

ISBN 0 7735 0127 4 (cloth)
ISBN 0 7735 0158 4 (paper)

LC 72 7846

Legal deposit 3rd quarter 1972

Design by Peter Maher

Printed in Canada by
T. H. Best Printing Company Limited

To my mother
who started me off
and my wife
who keeps me going

Contents

Acknowledgements

The poems on pages 1 and 165 are taken from *A Cardboard Garage*, copyright © 1969 by Clarke, Irwin and Company, Limited, by kind permission of the publishers.

Other portions and versions of this book have appeared in *The Tamarack Review*, *The Dalhousie Review*, *The University of Toronto Quarterly*, and *West Coast Review*.

This book has been published with the help of a grant from the Humanities Research Council of Canada, using funds provided by the Canada Council.

Brooding over chaos and the waste places
   He saw that it was bad.
His idle fingers swirled the jigsaw pieces
   Till he went mad.

Looking for bits with one straight edge to form
   His picture's border, he found none at all:
Only obscene curves quantified disorder.
   No green trees, no blue sky, no red-brick wall;

And even the dapple faded, year by year,
   To indeterminate greys and browns. But his hand
Still stirs the pieces round, his hooked eyes peer
   At the rubbed contours. Can't he understand

That there's no jigsaw? No mind ever fitted
   These scraps of card together, no fret cut
A pretty picture up. More to be mocked than pitied,
   All nails and pupils, he keeps his bed now. But

How long will nurses bring the pan? How long
   Will meals come up from the kitchen? Can he pay
For his private room for ever? And isn't it wrong
   To tie scarce facilities up this way?

His cracked gaze stirs the bits of his distress.
   He knows they won't fit,
But what else can he do? He would be in a worse mess
   If he solved it. . . .

Introduction
and Warning

'It is not by philosophy,' said Ambrose of Milan, 'that it has pleased God to save His people.' This was a piece of luck for Ambrose, who was no philosopher. He was perfectly right, of course: one would not expect to argue one's way into any heavenly mansion. But perhaps there is more than one way of being saved. To be saved is always to be saved from something, and different people may want to be saved from different things: from sin, from boredom, from a fate worse than death. And if we ask what people nowadays want to be saved from, it is not the worm that dieth not that leaps to mind. The object of fashionable dreads is *Angst*. In the interests of euphony, this term is sometimes rendered into English as Anxiety, but the translation misleads: it is rather a sense of meaninglessness. Hungry people are riddled with anxiety, but have no sense of the meaninglessness of their existence; they are saved from that by want of bread. People in no danger of hunger must look elsewhere for this salvation. In general, they do not have far to look. What takes away the danger of hunger is regular long-term employment, and most people with jobs look to those jobs for their own significance. Nothing could be more reasonable. Meaning depends on order, and what imposes order on the disjointed life of the city-dweller is the rhythm of his work. The more his job approximates to a career (and the further it gets from a mere flight from hunger) the more meaning it holds and can impart. This simple fact of life enrages some existential philosophers, who for some reason which is never made quite clear believe that such imparted meanings are evil: people, they say, are meaningless, and should feel that they are so and suffer from that feeling: giving

3

oneself a meaning is somehow cheating, like taking an aspirin when one ought to be having a headache. But, rage as they will, they know that people do in fact seek salvation from their *Angst* in their jobs.

A professional philosopher, then, must seek his salvation in philosophy. But what salvation can be found there? Salvation must be immune to doubt and question; but it is the philosopher's task, according to Thomas Aquinas, to call everything into question. One can of course call oneself a teacher or professor of philosophy, and organize one's existence around the teaching or professing of a fossilized dogma; but that is not to philosophize, and some at least of us would say that it is to teach something other than philosophy. Philosophy is the questioning of meanings and supposes no meanings. How then can it impart to the lives of its devotees the meaning that it necessarily lacks? If one tries to anchor one's wandering self in philosophy, all that happens is that philosophy breaks loose and floats away with one. The philosopher who seeks his salvation in his philosophy is thus in a quandary: if he gives his philosophy enough solid substance to serve the turn he deprives it of its nature as philosophy; and then, of course, it is no use.

The documents of which this book is made explore this quandary through successive refinements, ending in a reconciliation. It will already be obvious to the reader that, in such a quest, journey must be destination. What is not obvious is whether this condemns it to endless futility or endows it with perpetual significance.

There seem to be two ways of philosophizing. One way makes of philosophy a process of self-discovery; the other way makes of it an academic discipline. The latter, being academic and thus remote from vital concerns, seems unsuited to be a source of meaning for disordered lives. The former seems equally unsuited because it must receive order from the self it unfolds rather than impart an order of its own. One order cannot be got into life, the other must be got from it. Anyone who is determined to seek his salvation in philosophy must somehow find a way around this difficulty: a third way of philosophizing, or a way of showing that the two are the same or that one of the two does not suffer from the disability ascribed to it. And that is another way of describing the grail journey that this book logs.

An ambiguity has pervaded the paragraphs just written. Is this book an account of philosophy as a possible means to salvation or a record of one man's quest for his own salvation therein? The ambiguity cannot be resolved. On the one hand, the demands made of philosophy seem to be exorbitant: did we not say at the beginning that any career, just by being a career, could make a life meaningful? The extra demand made of philosophy must therefore be personal, reflect a personal need for relief from a personal self-mistrust. And the book certainly records the progress, even though a dialectical progress by bounce and rebounce, of an individual mind in its place and time. But on this showing, of course, it reduces to mere autobiography, of no philosophical interest. On the other hand, the book might be taken as a series of philosophical exercises arranged in a logical sequence. But what has such a sequence to do with being saved?

This ambiguity may be given another form: how sincere am I? Is the author laying bare his heart or just making a book? Certainly he is making a book, and every book is an artefact constructed like all artefacts in accordance with the inherent laws of its own being. That is a general truth that applies to philosophical books no less than to any others, although philosophers often try to conceal the fact by making their books badly: the demand for sincerity is a demand that can never be fulfilled, and that no intelligent critic makes. But surely a man's philosophy is unworthy of the name unless it is the expression of his whole personality, and how can it be that if it is not sincere? So one may well ask of such a book as this whether it is a sincere expression of opinion or a mere academic exercise. Unfortunately, once the question has been raised, the author cannot help to answer it. For his answer, should he offer one, would itself be part of the book, and subject to the same questioning. A man may insincerely avow sincerity, or sincerely declare himself insincere. To resolve the difficulty, each preface would have to be preceded by a further preface declaring how its successor was to be taken; and so to infinity. Thus the status of the whole must be left equivocal. However, at the end of the book an answer may be found implied, if not stated; and the problem turns out to be a commonplace, and its answer a cliché.

The equivocal nature of the present enterprise extends to the compilation of its parts. Is there a true sequence, a true log of the grail journey, or a mere collection of separate occasional pieces? Here at last is a question with a straightforward answer. Of the six prose pieces, the first, third and fourth were written for separate occasions without thought of each other. The second, written I don't know when or why, came to light one day while dusty files were sorted: perusal of it to discover its nature immediately revealed the order that combined the other three. The last two were written for their own occasions but also to complete the pattern that the first four left not quite complete. So the discovery of a partial, unintended pattern issued in deliberate completion of the pattern. Blind expressions of a need give place to willed fulfilment of the same need become desire. The story is, I should suppose, a commonplace one: most writers must often find that their work has taken on an unforeseen pattern. But, commonplace as the story may be, is it true? Can anyone ever truthfully say how he came to do what he has done, ever reliably sort out his memories of planning from his hindsights? And even if we accept this account of self-discovery giving place to self-making, is what was discovered and made the nature of a philosophical vocation or just the plan of a book?

One might have hoped to sort out what was merely personal from what was truly philosophical (or what was merely academic from what was truly human) by discriminating between what logic required and what will imposed. And certainly proofs prove, refutations refute, arguments have weight that may be pondered by all. But these are not enough by themselves to make a philosophy. They must be brought together and unified; and this unification may be effected either synthetically in the production of a philosophical work or organically in the manner of thought of a living man. Around and through the embattled logics move the winds of the spirit, blowing where they list. Every philosopher knows, though he may wish to forget, that other philosophers no less careful and competent than himself think other thoughts; and some philosophers at least know that when they write a book or an article what is written is partly what reason dictates, partly what the line of the chosen argument demands, and partly what the pattern of the literary product requires. The honest philosopher must therefore say: 'Hier steh' ich; ich könnt' aber anders'—here I stand, but I didn't have to.

Philosophy cannot divest itself of the personal, although there are familiar professional gestures that are by courtesy taken as representing such divestiture. Archimedes was wrong: to move the earth, it is not enough to have a place to stand. The place must be firmer than earth itself, and one must be firmly anchored there. Traditionally, such a standpoint is to be found in the professional methodologies of philosophical schools, and especially in the elaborations of systems. But the essence of such devices is to simplify; that is, to refuse to think much that one might have otherwise thought. Nietzsche therefore described 'the will to a system' as a philosopher's 'will to make himself out to be more stupid than he is.' 'I am not blinkered enough for a system,' he added; 'not even for my own system.'[1] Any system must inhibit the ceaseless quick play of the intelligence. Conclusions hold no more than their premises: mere inference is a poor substitute for new thought. So the call goes out for less system and more subtlety, less dogma and more invention. But what was just now said about the two ways of ordering thought suggests that this comes to the same thing as asking for more people and less books. Whatever is written tends to become systematic and therefore, in Nietzsche's eyes, stupid. And it is certainly true that in writing, though not in meditation and conversation, too great an elaboration, too careful a working of the surface, defeats itself. It anticipates, needlessly and irritatingly, the variety and subtlety of the readers' own thinking. What readers ask is something plain, even schematic, that they can work up into their own subtle and various truths. They need material for their own thinking, not a substitute for it. The qualifications and tergiversations of the living mind bore them, even bewilder them: when one is reading one can only take in what is a good deal stupider than one is oneself. So perhaps philosophers ought to be stupid, or to affect a stupidity that is not native to them. Does that mean that I, because I do not feel called upon to be any more stupid than I have to be, do not feel called upon to philosophize?

Once more we are plunged into equivocations. Is the author of this book philosophizing, or only talking about philosophizing? It has been a commonplace since Aristotle wrote his *Protrepticus* that the man who wonders whether to philosophize is already philosophizing (as is also the man who tries to show what is wrong with that argument), but perhaps even Aristotle would concede that such a man has his philosophical propensities fairly well under control. Philosophy or not, this book presents philosophy and the author as on mutual probation: the interest shown in the subject is at a high level of generality, and of a tentative character.

As to the generality of the interest, I suppose that an explanation is in order but no apology is required. The 'evils of specialization,' though little shunned, are much deplored. It is no bad thing that many should pursue their own lines of thought without a thought for the pattern those lines are making together: how else could the work of the mind go on? But it would be a pity if none or few were left to heed the pattern. It has been a fashion among scholars to praise specialist research to the dispraise of broad views, even to relegate the broad view to casual chat. Anyone, it is supposed, can discourse plausibly on large themes; it is minutiae that test a thinker's mettle. There is some truth in that, but it is no less true that the ignorant can be impressed by a parade of detailed learning enshrouding a depth of fatuity that would be at once evident were the matter in hand one of more general concern. And if it is true that broad views can be introduced into general talk where pedantry would be out of place, that is not because the former are trivial but because the latter is of no general interest. The fashion of which I speak is indeed more readily explained than defended. One would have thought that, especially in such times as ours when change in all realms of discovery and learning is continuous, deep, and swift, the establishment of mutual orientations should command attention as intent and scrupulous as any specialized research. But it is not so. The analogy of the microscope makes us confuse minuteness with precision, though woodsmen need naked eyes.

The defence of generality could serve as a plea for philosophy as such no less than for one unfashionable kind. After all, thinkers who give their minds to general orientations have no other name than philosophers. This has always been and remains philosophy's own province, however ill cultivated the province may be and whatever other provinces the discipline may have taken over. But the influence of academic fashion, together with the difficulty of raising a crop on the ancestral fields, has led even philosophers to abandon their embarrassing heritage and make specialists of themselves, working away at their professional preoccupations within a framework of assumptions that are not continually called in question. By substituting articles for books and notes for articles, and by judiciously refining one's technique at whatever length, one may so shorten the span of philosophical attention that the profounder implications of one's routine may never come to mind. Wisdom is justified of all her children, and since such refinement and such specialization are possible it is desirable that some should so specialize and refine; but it is desirable only on condition that others do not. To leave anything unquestioned, to pursue any inquiry without regard to its whole context (or rather, to all its possible contexts) is to court stupidity in some things so that one may be sharper about others, as a man using a telescope shuts out much of his vision in order to see some things in clear detail. Perhaps we were right to say that philosophers must be stupid; but, even so, is this their proper stupidity? If they have to be fools, may they not elect some other folly?

So much for the generality of the interest here taken in philosophy. To take philosophy itself as one's problem is to abstain from all of the problems that philosophers spend their working lives on. As for the tentativeness of the interest, it is from the very fullness and continuing presence of the sense that I might be doing or saying something quite different that this book arises. Its underlying question is: Can philosophy be shown to be necessary? And this question is echoed by another, fainter: Is philosophy necessary for me? But of course, these questions can only be reached by way of first asking: What is philosophy? And it is that question, in that form, that this book sets out to answer. But since, after all, it is a means of salvation that is sought, the question must also and more appositely be given the more personal form: What is philosophy for me? And since I who ask this am philosophizing in asking it, this question in turn becomes: What is philosophy *in* me? And this question at least admits of a definite answer. For this reason, the sentences that end 'The Central Problem of Philosophy' form a real conclusion not only to that essay but to the whole of the book up to that point. But that conclusion, as remarked before, is not an end of doubt but a reconciliation to doubting. —Can looking for philosophy really be itself a way of philosophizing? When one contemplates the product of those who think themselves to have found philosophy one is inclined to think that it may even be rather a good way.

One thing is still needed, if our search is not to end in perplexities as pervasive and paralysing as those in which it began: an undoubted reason for persisting in doubt. Happily, the question 'What is philosophy in me?' has yet a metamorphosis to undergo. Since I in asking it am philosophizing still, it may become: What is this philosophy, that I who practise it can ask continually what it is? And this question not only can be answered, but dictates its own answer: It is the activity in which a man becomes and remains problematical to himself. This answer, in its most general form, provides the theme of 'Speculation and Reflection.' And with that the quest is ended; it remains only to return us in 'Xanthippe' to the common condition of thinking and questioning humanity from which in 'Franciscus' we set out. Our questions have been given a final and definitive answer in the terms in which they were raised and in the setting that inspired them. If other terms and other settings might have imposed different solutions, that is no concern of ours.

Most of life and most of art is best enjoyed quietly. Philosophy in all its modes is a fine thing, and I am glad there are lots of people keeping it up; but Ambrose, though an administrator by nature and training, was not wholly mistaken. Must we for ever be explaining, and explaining, and explaining? Especially as our explanations are usually wrong.

Civilization begins in the great river valleys.

Franciscus

One July afternoon I walked out by the river, looking for Socrates. As I expected, I found him by the swimming-hole, his bald pate gleaming in the sun. All the boys, four or perhaps five of them, were in the water, splashing each other and shouting.

Socrates was in one of his trances and stood silent, his bulging eyes focused nowhere, his hands folded over his pot belly. While I waited for him to come round I walked up and down, peeling a stick and letting the bright scraps of bark fall here and there on the turf and on the scattered heaps of clothing.

After I suppose ten minutes one of the boys scrambled up on to the bank and began towelling himself vigorously. Socrates came out of his trance with a jerk. 'Water cold?' he inquired.

The boy evidently appreciated the nature of this gambit, but was too excited by something or other to pay any attention, or even to answer the question. Unable to restrain himself he burst out 'Tell me, Socrates, what is the difference between a man walking upstairs and a man looking up after him?'

Socrates reflected. 'Heracleitus used to say,' he observed at length, 'that the way up and the way down are one and the same. And Pythagoras, I remember, emphasized the superiority of the life of the spectator over that of the competitor. And though the man walking upstairs has no competitor, no doubt he endeavoured to find one and failed. We must not judge him too hardly on that score.'

Making a great effort to hide his disappointment, the boy persisted. 'Tell me then, Socrates,' he said, 'what is the difference between a duck?'

Socrates turned on him. 'That is a sophistical question,' he snapped, 'and rests upon an exploded fallacy. The question implies that as a duck the duck participates in being, but as a non-swan it participates in not-being; and that there can be no greater difference than that between being and not-being.' He turned to his secretary, who sat by him on a camp-stool, now as always taking down every word the Master uttered. 'Remind me to get into a dialogue about that some time.'

Seeing that the boy was becoming more and more irritated, and was indeed wondering whether he could run fast enough to risk kicking Socrates on the shins, I resolved to intervene. 'Look here, Socrates—' I began.

Socrates span round. 'Well, fancy meeting you!' he said. 'Let me introduce you. This young man is Francis. Francis, this gentleman is Mr Xenophon.' Encouraged by this introduction, inadequate though it was, I looked at the boy more closely. He seemed to be about twelve, and had untidy yellow hair which needed cutting, little piggy eyes, large ears and the supercilious yet trusting expression of the spoilt child. 'How typical of Socrates,' I thought. Out loud, I continued: 'Look here, Socrates, these questions Francis is asking you are riddles, not philosophy.'

'Riddles indeed,' replied Socrates, 'and very deep ones, since evidently I am unable to solve them to your satisfaction. But you say that they are not philosophy; and this intrigues me, for to know that they are not philosophy you must first know what philosophy is; and what philosophy is I have often wondered. What is it?'

Silence fell, broken at last by the boy Francis, who said 'I have a cousin who learned all about it at school, and my cousin says it's like nothing you ever heard before but you recognize it soon enough when someone starts talking it.'

Socrates was delighted. 'By the dog!' he said, 'this is the clearest case of Recollection ever I heard of. For how could you recognize what you never heard before, unless you had heard it in some previous existence?'

We readily agreed that this must be so.

'But let me bring to birth this knowledge with which you are pregnant,' Socrates went on. 'You are going to tell me what philosophy is. But tell me first, are all philosophers the same, or are some philosophers better than others?'

Francis said he didn't know.

'Well then, are all philosophers paid the same?'

'No indeed; for some are paid far more than the rest, and these they call "Professors." '

'And would a university pay a philosopher more money than it need?'

'Why, Socrates, what ridiculous questions you do ask.'

'Then some philosophers must be better than others, for otherwise no university would buy any but the cheapest variety.'

'Yes, some must be better than others.'

'Better at doing philosophy, or in some other respect?'

'At doing philosophy; for in no other respect can any superiority be discerned.'

'And who decides which are the good philosophers and which the bad?'

At this point the boy began to blush and stammer, for he was young and innocent; so I, with my greater knowledge of the world, came to his rescue. 'Surely, Socrates,' I said, 'you must know that it is the other philosophers. Not only do philosophers spend most of their days speaking well or ill of their colleagues, but when a university wishes to buy a philosopher, what does it do? It reads testimonials written for the candidate by philosophers of repute, and listens to advice from the philosophers it has already bought, and judges so.'

'Now at last,' said Socrates, 'I begin to see what philosophy is: philosophy is anything that a philosopher can persuade his colleagues to accept as such; and the criteria of philosophy, as I have long suspected but was ashamed to say until you emboldened me, are salary and celebrity. It follows that philosophy is in the main a compound of the arts of rhetoric and misthotic, of putting it across and of raking it in. He best philosophizes who persuades best and earns most.'

We were all a little saddened at this conclusion. Even the boys, who had finished their bathe and were listening, half-dressed and open-mouthed, stopped whispering and fell silent as though a funeral passed; for the glory of the intellect was tarnished before our eyes.

'Cheer up,' said Socrates at last, 'for there is a flaw in the argument with which we have chained the philosopher's soul, and perhaps if we apply all our energies we can set him free.'

While we were talking a friend of ours, a sleek fat smiling young man of about twenty-five, had come up along the tow-path and joined the group, and now broke in to ask 'What do you mean?'

'If we say that a philosopher is one who pleases other philosophers, whom did the first philosopher please?'

'Himself alone,' I replied.

'Now then,' Socrates went on, 'in what respect did he please himself? For many men ere this have pleased themselves, nay, set themselves rolling on the floor in rapture, yet they did not claim to be philosophers. So if we can find out what the first philosopher did to please himself, we shall perhaps find something which we can say is the true essence of philosophy.'

'But Socrates,' said Francis, 'how can we find out what the first philosopher did? He's dead, isn't he?'

'So what?' I interrupted. 'All the Primal Horde are dead, and left no written records; but did that prevent Freud from relating how the Primal Horde rebelled against its Patriarch? In a pig's eye.'

'Freud must have been guessing,' said Francis.

'We too can guess, you odd child,' said Socrates, smiling; 'and it may be that the second philosopher pleased the first philosopher in the same way that the first philosopher pleased himself, and so on till the present day when the n-plus-first philosopher pleases the nth. So tell me, how do philosophers test those who wish to become philosophers?'

'They set them exams, I expect,' said Francis.

'And how,' Socrates went on, turning to me, 'do Professors test the philosophers their universities wish to buy?'

'They interview them.'

'And what have these two processes in common?'

Francis and I were silent; but, while we pondered, the friend who had intervened before answered for us. 'I suppose it's just that in both the candidate answers questions.'

'I knew it!' cried Socrates. 'Thank you, Maurice; for now I see that doing philosophy is answering questions; and the man who is best at answering them is acknowledged to be the best philosopher. Only,' he continued, 'what sort of questions?'

'That's hard to say' said Maurice, with the tone of one who does not find it at all hard to say anything; 'but they're not the ordinary sort of questions you can find the answer to. For when I was writing my dissertation on the methods of the social sciences I always found that when I made a statement that could be verified, or asked a question for which the method of finding an answer could be laid down, my supervisor would tell me that that question or that statement was no part of philosophy but belonged to one of the positive sciences.'

'Yes,' I said, 'I remember you telling us, Maurice, that what made the distinction between the sciences was the different techniques of solution they adopted, and that was what made you choose that topic for your thesis. What, then, is the method of philosophy? Why not write next upon the technique of answering philosophical questions?'

Socrates while we spoke had put on an expression of deep thought, and now said: 'This reminds me of a dream I once had. In that dream the growth of science was revealed to me. When men began to wonder what the sky is made of, and why rivers run downhill, and whether the earth is flat and the will free, and what makes men shiver when they have the ague, they knew how to solve none of these problems; and so, instead of finding out what *was* the case, they reasoned and disputed about what *must be* the case; and this they called philosophy. But as soon as they found a method by which a group of these problems might be solved they ceased to argue about what must be so and joined together in discovering what really was so. And to each group of questions for the solution of which the same method was used, they gave the name of "a science"; and to the residue of still rebarbative questions and the arguments by which they still hoped in vain to find a solution, they still gave the name of "philosophy." And in my dream I saw a vision which made me sweat and groan: for I saw the first good number made flat and then solid to give it power over the lives of men, and applied three times to the generations of men that shall have passed from my birth;[1] and at that time I saw that means were known to solve all the questions that trouble reasonable men to answer them. And this pleased me till I saw that to the evil scourings of curiosity the divine name of PHILOSOPHY was still given, and that the evil scourings of the learned world rooted among the garbage and grew fat thereon.'

Maurice spoke more quietly then, for he saw that Socrates was deeply moved, but he continued: 'Yes, philosophy has no method; no philosopher knows what he is about, and if he did know he would stop. For how does any philosopher criticize those of a previous generation? He shows that the method they used was neither that which they supposed themselves to be using nor that which the tasks they had set themselves demanded. Yet few philosophers ask themselves whether their own methods are adequate to the tasks they suppose themselves to be performing; and if any asks, he gets no comforting answer. And here is another thing, Socrates, from which you can see that there is no agreed method of settling philosophical disputes: if there were, there would be agreed solutions to philosophical questions. For what makes a science possible? Chiefly this, that by agreed methods agreed solutions are reached. And to philosophical questions there are no agreed solutions.'

Silence fell. Then Socrates asked in a low voice: 'So philosophy has no method?'

'It has none, Socrates.'

'Then it is not a science?'

'No.'

'Then,' Francis burst in impatiently, 'whatever is it?'

'What is there left for it to be?' replied Socrates. 'It can only be a knack or a trick. And I suppose it is the knack or trick of dealing convincingly and lucratively with problems for whose solution no satisfactory technique has been devised.'

Socrates then relapsed into a prolonged meditation and, seeing that some sort of finality had been achieved, all the boys except Francis went away, leapfrogging as they went and blowing on blades of grass which they held between their thumbs so that they made a blurting noise. The secretary sharpened his pencils and got up to stretch his legs, while Maurice and I looked at each other glumly. Socrates lifted his head and smiled at us. 'Don't be downhearted,' he said, 'for not all dreams are from the gate of horn; philosophy, the mother of the sciences, is not yet past bearing, and the world is young.' He hesitated for a minute and, when his secretary returned from the shrubbery, continued: 'Do you remember saying that riddles were not philosophy? Well, now we know what philosophy is, but not what riddles are. What are they?'

'They are a sort of question,' I answered.

'Is there any agreed method of solving them?'

'No,' put in Francis. 'That's the whole point.'

'Then riddles are philosophy,' said Socrates, 'or at least the study of riddles is. So let us study them. Now, how shall we begin?'

'Francis asks riddles from morning till night,' said Maurice. 'Ask him.'

'A riddle is a sort of question, isn't it?' asked Socrates.

'Yes,' said Francis.

'What sort?'

'I'll show you,' said Francis. 'You remember the method of Division you showed me the other day? Well, I've tried it out on riddles.'

'Show us,' I said.

'But remember,' Maurice warned him, 'this method of Division has no scientific status. If you know that a this is a sort of a that, and want to know what sort, it will help you to get clear; but that doesn't mean that the sort was a real sort before you found it in your Division. Isn't that right, Socrates?'

'Yes,' said Socrates, 'it imposes an order on nature and does not discover the order which nature keeps hidden in her heart. —At least, not unless performed by an expert like Maurice here. And its use is that of a small-scale map which shows you where you are in the world, not that of a large-scale map which shows you what the surrounding country is like. But let Francis get on with it, if he doesn't mind.'

Francis led us down to the drinking-place where the cattle had trodden a broad spit of sandy soil into the slow waters of the Tone; he smoothed it out with his toes and drew on it this diagram with a stick, talking as he drew:

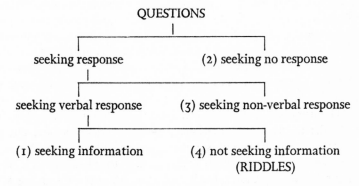

'The first sort are the obvious ordinary sort of questions like "What is the capital of Australia?" asked by someone who really wants to know. An example of the second sort, those that seek no response, would be this. If when I came out of the river just now I'd forgotten where I had left my clothes and exclaimed angrily "Where in Hell did I leave my towel?", this would be merely a verbal equivalent for action in searching and would seek no response, unless I meant my remark to quell your suspicions that I might be seeking someone else's towel. A little later if my search had been unsuccessful I might have exclaimed "Why was I born such a fool?" and this would be a mere exclamation and certainly require no response at all. But I'd like you to notice that not all rhetorical questions fall into this second class; many belong to the third class, of questions not asking for information on what seems to be their subject, and seeking a response that is not (or not primarily) verbal. What is the function of a rhetorical question? Sometimes it is to implicate an audience in a speaker's views. If an orator said "The British Empire has gone to pot" his audience might repudiate the statement angrily. But if he asked, with a catch in his melodious voice, "Where is that mighty Empire today?" what would happen?'

'The audience,' I said, 'will think to themselves: "Alas! it has gone to pot." '

'Thank you,' Francis resumed, 'but I meant that for a rhetorical question. But you're right, they will think so, and they will not be angry with the speaker for saying it; because it is not he who has said it. Questions more clearly requiring non-verbal responses are, however, such questions as "Do you know the time?" and "Would you mind passing the salt?" To answer *yes* to the former and *no* to the latter is inadequate.'

'I was walking down by the Market the other day,' I said, 'when an old man came up and said "Excuse me, can you tell me the way to the Castle?" I said "Yes" and after waiting a few moments he walked away, muttering. Suddenly I felt ashamed and rushed after him. "I'm sorry I was so rude just now," I said; "please forgive me. You want to know the way to the Castle, don't you?" "No," replied the old man.'

'The story is old,' said Francis, 'but the idea is correct. —Lastly we have the fourth class, questions seeking a verbal response but not requesting information. It is to this class that riddles belong.'

I asked if they were the only members of the class. Francis said he didn't know, he hadn't really thought. Maurice, refraining with obvious difficulty from making the obvious comment, said: 'Yes, of course there are others. What about what one used to do at school, mental arithmetic for example? You can't tell me the teacher needed to know what nineteen nineteens are. Questions asked by school-teachers belong to your fourth class, and in a way they're quite like riddles. They have only one right answer; and the purpose of the question is simply to find out whether you know what that right answer is. If you think about it, that's the chief point of a riddle, to find out if you know what the right answer is.'

'That only applies to some riddles,' said Francis, nettled, 'and then only on a very superficial level. I'd better tell you what the seven types of riddle are, then you'll see.'

No one made any very encouraging sound, but without obvious signs of embarrassment the child continued. 'The primitive riddle,' he began, 'offers a concealed description of something. The answerer has to name what is being described. Usually there is a bet on the result. Riddling of this sort is a solemn business, a serious ritual. You remember the Sphinx made all comers bet their lives that they knew what began with four legs, then had two and ended with three. At last Oedipus said it was a man; the Sphinx lost the bet and her life. And you remember the riddles Gollum asked the Hobbit.'

'I do *not* remember,' said Maurice, 'but never mind.'

'A point about this type of riddle,' Francis went on, never minding, 'is that a sharp-witted man can answer right even if he has never heard the riddle before.

'That's type one. The other types become possible only when people get used to answering riddles. It is the prevalence of the riddling habit that gives people the confidence to look for answers to what seem to be crazy questions. Once the habit and the confidence become established, one can exploit them by asking questions with trick answers. So there grew up a second type of riddle, the kind that is commonest nowadays, that depends on puns. These are what they call conundrums, and they came in with euphuism. For example, *What is the difference between a drainpipe and a stupid Dutchman?* —*One's a hollow cylinder and the other's a silly Hollander.* Some of these can be answered (as with type one) by an astute person who has not heard them before, but usually we meet them too young for this to be feasible.

'The remaining types are parasitic upon these two. The second type increases the confidence that the first type has engendered, by using stereotyped forms—*Why is* A *like* B? *What is the difference between* A *and* B?—that make it unnecessary to say "Here is a riddle" every time. The third type of riddle depends upon these set forms and the confidence they create. It distorts the forms so that the answer cannot be guessed, because the question asks nothing and usually the answer is irrelevant as well. Examples are *What is the difference between a duck?* (to which the answer, Socrates, is *One of its legs is both the same*) and *Why is a mouse when it spins?*— *Because the higher the fewer.* Thus a feeling of confidence conflicts with a feeling of helplessness, to the confusion of the answerer and the delight of the poser.

'In the next type, the fourth, the question appears to expect a normal response, but in fact does not. For instance, *Why is Winston Churchill like Father Christmas?* is answered, not as one would expect by a pun, but by *They both have beards, except Winston Churchill.*

'There are three types of riddle left. In all of them, the fact that a conundrum has a stereotyped response is used to betray the answerer. In the next two it is used to embarrass him as well. The fifth type exploits the conventional admission of ignorance: *What is the difference between a piano and your face?—I don't know—A piano makes music but your face makes me sick*; or *What is the difference between a laundry, an undertaker and a pin?—I don't know—A laundry stiffens the collars and an undertaker collars the stiff 'uns—What about the pin?—That's the point*. Some of this kind can be evaded by not answering in the set forms designed to elicit the correct answer from the poser. In extreme cases, indeed, the trick works only within a very narrow convention: *What is the difference between a man going upstairs and a man looking up after him and the Torbay Express?—I don't know—The first is stepping upstairs and the second is staring up steps*. Then the answerer has to ask *But where does the Torbay Express come in?* so that the poser can reply *It comes in at Paddington Station*.

'The sixth type, the other kind which can be used to embarrass, cannot be evaded by using this set form, and can be met only by refusing to answer. These pose dilemmas: *Does your head ring?—Yes* being answered by *That shows it's hollow* and *No* by *That shows it's cracked*. James Joyce has a refined specimen. A small boy is asked *Do you kiss your mother when you go to bed?* His answer is repeated publicly: *Here's a boy says he kisses/doesn't kiss his mother when he goes to bed*. The sole purpose of this is to elicit a pronouncement on a subject supposedly embarrassing to a small boy.'

'Power through possession of personal property,' said Maurice. 'Never leave nail-clippings lying about, a witch might get them and work a magic on you. If you know Rumpelstiltskin's name you have power over him. A personal fact is personal property. The children were playing black magic.'

'I don't know about that,' said Francis, 'but the seventh and last type is parasitic on the rest, and relies on the sophisticated answerer's ignorance as to what type the riddle belongs to. *Fifty people got on an empty train. At the first station, ten got off and nineteen got on; at the next station fifty-nine got off and one got on; at the next none got off and three got on*. Then if the answerer has not appeared to be calculating you ask *How many people are left on the train?* and if you think he has calculated you say *What was the name of the engine-driver?* and his work has gone for nothing.'

'What *was* the name of the engine-driver?' I asked.

'Smith.'

'Why Smith?'

'Because his father's name was Smith' said the child smugly.

Maurice looked at me. I cleared my throat and said loudly 'Well, Socrates, what did you think of that performance?'

There was no answer. We looked round. Socrates had gone into another trance, this time flat on his back, his eyes shut, and his rough stonemason's hands folded on his gently heaving abdomen. We decided to leave him out of it.

'It wasn't bad as far as it went,' said Maurice, 'but I think I can isolate an eighth type of riddle.'

'You do, do you?' said Francis. 'Go on then, try.'

'All right,' said Maurice, 'I mean those where you know the substance of the answer but not the form. We come close to it in this example: *The letters of the alphabet were asked out. Six were late. Which?* You know it must be some set of letters, but have nothing to go on in deciding which set. You don't know what is being asked: you don't know what "coming late" means as applied to letters.'

'I see,' I said. 'You mean that "A and B came late" is meaningless, either because it is in principle unverifiable or because the logical grammar of letters of the alphabet disqualifies them from coming late.'

"No I don't,' said Maurice, 'why bring that up? The logic of riddling is not the logic of science or practical life. "Coming late" has in this instance a perfectly definite meaning. It means, as it usually does, coming after some standard—in this case coming after *T*, and the answer is *U V W X Y* and *Z*. But to stop you vapouring about logical grammar, here is a proper example of what I had in mind. *How many beans make five?*'

'I see now,' I said; 'you mean, we know the answer is five, but that's too easy and we don't know how it should be put.'[2]

'*A bean and a half and half a bean and half a bean and a half,*' said Francis.

'But that makes three! Oh no, I get it. How feeble. But that reminds me,' I said, 'of another kind of question, though it isn't a riddle. When a man asks you "Have you heard the one about the Englishman, the Irishman and the Scotsman?" you can't answer till you know which one of the innumerable stories on that topic it is to be.'

'That is a question seeking a non-verbal response,' Francis replied; 'he doesn't want an answer at all. All he means is "I'm going to tell

you the one about the Englishman, the Irishman and the Scotsman."
He is trying to arouse your expectation and appetite. The answer
"Yes" would surprise and hurt him.'

'Even in conundrums,' said Maurice, 'the question form is not
essential. The only reason for not saying "A door is not a door when
it's a jar" is that the question form arouses what you call "expectation
and appetite"—in a word, suspense. Cross-talk comedians often
distribute question and answer differently: *I bought some today, but
they wouldn't strike on the box!—What wouldn't?—Kippers.*'

'Inessential they may be,' I said, 'but the standard forms of riddle
question are odd, aren't they? *Why is A like B? What is the difference
between A and B?* There may be a hundred likenesses and differences,
but we're asked for *the* difference. There's only one right answer,
and we recognize it when we hear it. How is this? How can we expect
to know what the unique difference is?'

'Before you can answer a riddle of that sort,' said Maurice, 'you
must ask yourself a preliminary question: "In what universe of
discourse is there one and only one analogy (positive or negative)
between A and B?" *What is the difference between a buffalo and a
bison?* In the world of fact there are many differences or none, so we
transfer our attention to the world of words: at once we see the
answer—*Yer can wash yer 'ands and fice in a bisin.* Riddles in this
form commit the fallacy of "many questions." If there is more than
one universe of discourse in which a unique analogy can be found,
the riddle has more than one answer and is unfair.'

'What,' said Francis, 'is a universe of discourse?'

'If your head's empty,' said Maurice, 'keep it shut so it doesn't
show.'

I regretted Maurice's relapse from his hard-won maturity, as I did
not know myself what a universe of discourse was, nor indeed
exactly what was meant by positive and negative analogies, though
of course I knew the riddle about the bison. So I quickly changed the
subject. 'When I was about your age,' I said to Francis, 'I was greatly
puzzled by this problem. Suppose you had a trunk full of postage
stamps, so full that you couldn't get any more in. Could you get one
more stamp in, or would it stop the lid from shutting? I never could
understand why no one else was bothered by this question; they
said, of course you couldn't. I can see it now, but I'm still not easy
about it.'

'Excellent!' said Maurice. 'Really a classical case of philosophical
puzzlement! I wouldn't mind betting that your trouble was that you

were thinking in pictures, and the pictures were inappropriate. The form of the question helps: you had a trunk full already, and shut; one more, and it stopped the lid from shutting. That suggests a contrast between easy shutting and not shutting at all, which seems incommensurate with the small difference in the trunk's contents. But the other people you asked—more experienced people, I imagine —conjured up more suitable images. If it was really so full that *no* more stamps could be got in, very great force would already have to be applied to close it. It would creak and groan, you would expect it to collapse under the strain any moment. One more stamp, and the hinges would go. It was touch and go before; so the single extra stamp didn't make all that difference.'

I was glad to see Maurice restored to good humour by this demonstration of his superiority and, though I could not see that he had done anything at all to clear up the trouble about the stamps, I judged it was now safe to return to the problem which really interested me. 'Thank you, Maurice,' I said, 'that makes it perfectly clear. But I still don't see just why, in a riddle, we can talk about *the* difference. Why are we so sure there is only the one answer?'

'I can tell you that,' said Francis. 'Indeed, I already have. Riddling is a ritual. Think of the catechism.'

'The question form isn't essential there, either,' said Maurice. 'Any catechism seems much the same sort of thing as any set of versicles and responses. The swing of the antiphony has a hypnotic effect. There *must* be a response, or the rhythm will be broken.'

'But in a riddle,' I protested, 'you have no rhythm. There is only the single question and answer.'

'Yes, yes,' said Francis, 'don't be awkward. The point is that riddles have a ritual aspect, which I dare say is enhanced by all these parallels. The set form of the question tells you what sort of a question it is. Habit makes you respond.'

'Rhythm is only accelerated habit,' Maurice put in. He liked to be oracular. We let it pass. Maurice tried again. 'The force of habit has something of the same effect in philosophy,' he said. 'An expression like "causation" or "free will" sets the philosopher's tongue in a groove, and he goes right through the catechism. All those famous problems of philosophy have their own momentum. Perhaps there has been no real problem for centuries, but we know what Hume said and what he found difficult and we continue to ask our questions in the form he gave them.'

'Doesn't the potency of habit and ritual break down,' I said, trying to bring the conversation back to a level on which I could keep up with it, 'in the one about the engine-driver? The point of that was, if I remember, that the answerer might not be impelled by these forces to do the mental arithmetic, and the poser is prepared to handle him either way.'

'Well, yes,' Francis explained, 'but it's no fun if he doesn't mind admitting that he didn't do the sum. It's only fun if he's embarrassed.'

'You see?' said Maurice. 'Shame is a sanction still. And sanction plays a big part in riddles of the first type. For failing to answer the Sphinx, the sanction was death. More usually, if Francis is right, there is a cash wager.'

'Of course I'm right,' said Francis. 'Even if you never heard of Bilbo Baggins, there's Samson. He bet thirty sheets and thirty change of garments they couldn't guess it, but they got his wife to tell them: *Out of the eater came forth meat, and out of the strong came forth sweetness—What is sweeter than honey? And what is stronger than a lion?*'

Maurice made the astonishing admission that he had forgotten about Samson, but at once made it plain that he could afford to concede a point as he was about to go one better. 'Samson had another riddle,' he said: '*What makes me strong?* They got the answer to that one from a woman, too; the sanction was his strength, his sight and his freedom. In both cases, Samson made trouble later. But like Stephen Dedalus and Rumpelstiltskin, in his second riddle he gave away a personal secret. As I said before, if a witch gets clippings of your nails and hair you are in the witch's power.'

'Passwords and so on are like the Sphinx's riddle,' said Francis. 'If you don't answer the sentry right he may shoot. To demand the password is to ask a question seeking a verbal response that provides no information about its ostensible subject matter; there's only one right answer, which can't be guessed but must be known; and the sanction is death.'

'And sometimes they belong to my eighth type,' rejoined Maurice. 'When the Japanese infiltrated into Malaya we had to screen them. We'd line up all the men in a village and make them say "alleluiah." If they did, all right. But the Nips could only say "arreruiah." They knew the substance, but not the form. And the sanction was loss of freedom, perhaps of life.'

'What about this for a type-six riddle, a dilemma one?' I said, determined not to be left out. 'A man was challenged by a sentry: "Halt!" The man halted. The sentry said "Halt!" again. "Well, I halted," said the man; "What's wrong?" "Nothing's wrong," said the sentry: "my orders are, to shout *halt* three times and then fire. Halt!" '

'That's the first sensible thing you've said this afternoon,' said Maurice. 'If he halts he's shot, if he doesn't halt he's shot.'

I was encouraged to continue. 'People used to say that science consists of putting questions to Nature and forcing her to give the answers. Now, what would be the sanction there, do you suppose?'

'That's easy,' said Maurice: 'accusations of irrationality. As you and Socrates were saying, the normal way of testing someone is by a series of questions. Thus Nature's rationality is tested by a series of questions which she has to answer. I think it's quite true that for science a question without an answer doesn't count, and neither does an answer without a question. Or so Campbell says.'[3]

'What do you mean, an answer without a question?'

'Well, take Soal's work on card-guessing. The work looks all right, but they don't know what questions it answers, so they don't allow it to count as science.'

'So on the whole,' I said, 'it looks as if the question-and-answer and versicle-with-response that are so prominent in riddling are important in real life too; and in philosophy as well, I should imagine. Most philosophers' questions aren't worth answering, for everyday purposes. But some people feel that they have to answer them, and that there must in each case be a right answer—if only they could find it.'

'Yes,' said Maurice, 'that's the compulsive force of the form, and it comes from ritual. No ritual is more powerful here than that of the examinations that all aspiring philosophers sit so often. "ALL questions must be answered," the papers keep saying. The fashion for radio quizzes and so on has the same effect. The bright man is the one who comes up quickly with the approved answer. The man who has the sense not to try to answer at all fares less well.'

'There's a big difference, though, isn't there,' said Francis, 'between riddles and exams and quizzes and so on, and philosophy.'

I was shocked. 'What do you mean?' I exclaimed. 'Didn't you hear Socrates prove that riddles *are* philosophy?'

'Who cares what Socrates proves?' said Francis. 'In riddles and the like, the poser knows the answer already. In fact, the answer is probably made up before the riddle: you think up a pun and say, "I could make a riddle out of that." That must have happened with the old one about the ships who got married. The answer is: *One married ridiculously, she got tied to a buoy; one presumptuously, she made up to a pier; one foolishly, she anchored after a heavy swell; and one wisely, she was tender to a man of war.* The whole thing is a monument of Victorian industry, but to ask it so that it sounds like a riddle is next to impossible. That's nearly an answer without a question; but surely the philosopher doesn't know the answers to the questions he asks?'

'Of course he doesn't,' Maurice replied. 'That was the point of Socrates' dream. The questions philosophers ask nowadays have no answers. That's why people have gone on asking them for centuries without ever getting an answer. A man who asks *What is substance?* or *What is the nature of life?* isn't asking anything, really. He's just making an interrogative noise and is hypnotized by the force of ritual into supposing that there must be an answer for it.—Just like Lewis Carroll asking *Why is a raven like a writing-desk?* and then feeling obliged to invent some kind of an answer. But the philosopher is in worse case, because he has *really* fooled himself. All you can do for the poor fellow is to keep explaining very loudly and clearly that there is no answer because there is no question, and hope that common sense will at last seep in. An interrogative noise cannot be satisfactorily answered except by a comforting grunt.'

We all acquiesced in this. But then something happened that amazed us all. Emboldened by the droning and snorting that testified to the depth of Socrates' trance, his silent secretary joined the conversation. 'I say,' he said, 'we can't have this, you know.'

We looked at him. 'What *do* you mean?' said Maurice.

The secretary flushed a deep red, swallowed and said 'Look. You're sawing away your own perch. You and your friends are always speaking contemptuously about "philosophy" and "philosophers," as though they were terms of abuse. Why don't you say "those philosophers who disagree with us," which is what you mean? You're all philosophers; at least, you take money for being so. But of course you mean to imply that you yourselves aren't philosophers *really*; *really*, you are scientists and men of affairs who in your spare time throw off chance remarks which happen to be easily mistaken for philosophy. You are always sneering at "theorists," too. You yourselves aren't theorists, oh no, you're sternly practical men in business suits with no abstract nonsense about you. Let me assure you, to the rest of us you look and sound just like all the other philosophers, only less honest. You make me sick.'

'Unlike the piano,' said Maurice, who surprised me by keeping his temper. 'You've got us wrong: really, we aren't philosophers. Philosophy is dead, and we are the undertakers.—No, we're the executors, winding up the bankrupt estate. We aren't theorists, either; we just destroy the theories other people build.'

'Philosophy isn't dead,' said the secretary.

'Prove it.'

'I can't prove it, but I'll try to convince you.' He turned to Francis. 'There's something common to almost all the types of question you distinguished.'

'Of course there is,' said Francis: 'they're all questions. I mean, they're all things you'd expect to find a question mark at the end of. What did you have in mind?'

' "They all seek a response" is the way you'd put it,' said the scribe. 'But I prefer it this way: they are all requests for something. No question should ever be dismissed as "silly"—that's a lazy way out. A man who asks "What is substance?" wants something, and something worth having, though he may not be certain what it is he wants. People aren't *merely* silly: silliness is just sense that needs a bit of straightening. Of course, people who ask questions like that may be not well-meaning and muddled but clear-headed and malicious. I read a book once whose author said he didn't want to answer the question "Do you know that the world has existed for some time?" by saying "Well, if you mean this I do, if you mean that I don't, if you mean the other I'm not sure but I think it's probable," for fear of sounding foolish.[4] His imagination failed him there, for that is the best sort of answer to that sort of question. What would a man be after if he asked a question like that? Obviously not information. The odds are that he is leading up to something, trying to trap us into agreeing to something we won't want to. So the right thing to do is to dodge the trap, and what keeps people out of traps is caution. So the cautious answer was the right one, and it would only sound foolish to someone who didn't realize what was going on. If that author had only talked to my boss for a bit, he'd have recognized the technique. But where was I?'

A pause followed as we tried to remember what he had been setting out to prove. 'I've got it!' said Francis suddenly. 'You were going to say that a man who asks *What is substance?* really has a problem of some sort.'

'That's it,' said the secretary. 'It isn't a silly question, merely a misleading one. What you have to do is not to get him to feel that he has no problem, but to help him to find out what it is that he really wants. Then you have to satisfy his need, whatever it may be. Socrates' dream misled him, you can see how.'

'Yes, I see what you mean' said Maurice, and Francis nodded.

'I can't,' I said.

Francis said, 'It assumed that as soon as the questioner knew what he wanted he would stop wanting it.'

'Yes,' Maurice agreed, 'it's what we used to call the therapeutic method. We tried to cure people of a complaint called "philosophical puzzlement." As a psychoanalyst cures his patient by talking to him and letting him talk, so "The sophist effects a change from the worse to the better condition by discourse."[5] But were we right to suppose that there were no questions that would need answering when all those cramping perplexities had been soothed away? Perhaps we have let ourselves be fascinated by the idea of a technique of solution.'

'I see,' I said. 'I suppose that was what Socrates was thinking of when he said perhaps philosophy wasn't done for after all.'

'There's more to it than that,' said the secretary. 'Don't you see that they make an assumption that's obviously false?'

This baffled us all. 'Who? What? How?' we said dispersedly.

'Well, look,' he went on, 'how can there be isolated questions?'

'I may be wrong,' I retorted, 'but it seems to me that what you just asked was one.'

'Not so isolated as all that. It occurred in the context of our talking and thinking together. And it grew from the soil of my life and thought. And besides, it was framed in the English language. I didn't specially invent the words for it, or the affinities that made it possible to fit them together in that way and be understood. In every question you ask, the accumulated experience of all the generations who spoke English before you is latent. And in any case, no philosopher has ever tried to deal with questions in isolation—in such isolation, that is, as they could have. He tries to effect a synthesis.'

Maurice laughed at this, rather rudely, I thought. 'I suppose you are going to say that the philosopher accepts all the conclusions of all the sciences and uses them as the foundation of a sort of super-scientific world-picture,' he said. 'It takes the average genius all his time to keep up with one branch of one of the sciences.'

'That would be ridiculous humbug,' said the secretary, 'and I have at least been with Socrates long enough to know that philosophy and humbug are incompatible. It isn't that at all. Philosophy doesn't need an elaborate factual basis. You're still letting the glories of science dazzle you. Systematic philosophy isn't more than science, it's different from science. It proceeds by argument, not by investigation, as Socrates saw it in his dream. Its function is not to provide extra information about the world. It doesn't settle what is true, but what it would be most convenient to say.'

'Pragmatist!' I said.

'If this be pragmatism, make the most of it. I'm not frightened by names. But it isn't. Pragmatism is a theory about truth, in science or anywhere. What I'm saying is that philosophy has nothing to do with truth at all. Even Aristotle knew you couldn't arrive at the truth by dialectic.'

'Then what's the good of it, if it's nothing to do with truth?' said Francis.

'You tell me,' returned the secretary. 'What's the good of mental arithmetic?'

'I suppose it makes you quick, and makes sure you really know your tables.'

'Exactly! Only I put it this way, mental arithmetic functions as a rehearsal. You rehearse your reactions, and so prepare for later life when you'll need to be quick and accurate and react right first time when someone asks you for change.'

'The rehearsed response becomes the habitual response,' said Maurice, 'and saves you the trouble of counting on your fingers each time.'

'Exactly! Exactly! And isn't that what philosophy does?'

'How?' said Maurice.

'I'm just going to tell you. A system of ethics or metaphysics organizes your reactions. Instead of having to work out the answer to each question on its merits, by counting up on your fingers, you give the answer your tables give, the answer according to your system, without hesitation. In acquiring such a system you rehearse your reactions to situations you may meet later, only situations much more varied than mental arithmetic helps in. When you have no time or opportunity to find the right answer to a question, a metaphysical system enables you to say something that will harmonize with the rest of your beliefs. And if a question has no "right" answer (as you would say) because it has no fixed meaning, the system will fix its meaning and within the context of the system there will be a right answer. What is the result? Comfort, orientation! A feeling that you are at home in the world! In a word, coherent living. What savages have because they refrain from thought, philosophers get from their thinking. And on top of all this, every philosopher knows how often habits of speech lead him astray. By deliberately adopting a system, you organize your speech habits so that they become a help and not a burden.'

'So philosophy is just a way of talking?' said Maurice.

'A way of talking, a way of thinking, a way of living, what's the difference?' cried the secretary, who by this time was quite helpless before the torrent of his own ideas. 'We think in words, thinking is talking; and a word may be the sufficient stimulus of a consequential action, so a way of talking is a way of living.'

'So then you don't agree with Socrates about philosophy being the art of dealing with questions for whose solution no method has been found?' I asked him.

'Yes, why not?—up to a point. But there may still be a right and a wrong way of dealing with such questions. And about that business of method in science, I remember your Mr. Campbell saying that what he liked about physics was just this, that there wasn't any method of devising experiments, you had to use your own unaided ingenuity and experience. Well, I dare say that's not the point. The real mistake was to think that you could talk in terms of isolated questions. That isn't so: the system comes first, and doesn't necessarily start by answering any one particular question. Between you and me, this obsession with isolated questions is the reason poor old Socrates never got far enough on with his philosophy to get himself a job. You don't want to pay any attention to that dream of his; it's only sour grapes.

'But of course he isn't consistent. You remember that row he had with Euthydemus? There, it was Euthydemus who stuck to the single question and answer, well he was talking in riddles really, and Socrates got very angry and tried to start a proper discussion that would build up to something. I really thought then that he'd reformed. But no, when he met Protagoras he was at it again, one question one answer or I won't play, and as soon as Protagoras tried to introduce some sense into the discussion he choked him off. The trouble with the boss is, he can't make up his mind what he wants.'

In his excitement he had failed to notice what Maurice and I had both seen during this last speech, that Socrates had come out of his trance. I never admired Socrates' character more than I did then. Without a sound he had closed his eyes again; and now he yawned noisily and sat up. 'Dear me,' he said, 'I must have dropped off. The last thing I heard was your analysis of the seven types of riddles,

Francis; I enjoyed that very much.' While Francis caught my eye and giggled, Socrates turned to his secretary and continued: 'Did they say anything interesting after that?'

'We decided,' I broke in, 'that you can't answer questions in isolation, you have to have a system.'

'Oh, really?' said Socrates. 'How very interesting. And does this system help you to answer questions you would otherwise have asked in isolation?'

'Yes, it does.'

'And might these questions not have been answered by some other method?'

'Not all of them, Socrates. Some of them would be meaningless outside the system.'

'Then the system can take little credit for answering them.'

'I suppose not.'

'And some of the questions might be answered outside the system?'

'Yes.'

'And would the system give the same answer as the direct method?'

'I don't know, I suppose it would.'

'But how do you know it would?'

'I said, I don't know, perhaps it wouldn't.'

'And if they differ, which is right?'

'I don't know.'

'Is a general system likely to give a more accurate result than an investigation whose special methods are entirely devised to meet the needs of the particular situation?'

'It seems hardly likely.'

'So a philosophical system is an easy way of finding wrong answers to questions for which it would be hard to find the right answers?'

'I suppose it must be.'

'So,' said Socrates, 'perhaps it was of your systems that the poet was thinking when he prayed to be delivered "from all the easy speeches that comfort cruel men." '

'But look here,' said Maurice, 'if the answers differ, how can you tell which is right except by referring them back to some system?'

'It would take a long time to work that one out,' said Socrates, 'and Francis here is late for his supper already. But at least I can take it that what you said when I was asleep contradicts what we said when I was awake?'

'Yes' I agreed.

'In the light of new knowledge gleaned from the talk about riddles?'

'Not really,' I confessed, 'the argument just seemed to run that way.'

'Then if what you said after you had said before, you would have said after what you now said before?'

'Come again?'

'If you had started by advocating systems you might have ended by favouring single questions, since no new knowledge made you change from one position to the other.'

'I suppose that's possible,' I agreed.

'Beware, then, of supposing that what is later is necessarily better.'

'Well,' interposed Maurice briskly, 'I enjoyed that very much. What say we drop round to the Cross Keys for the odd pint?'

'Excellent suggestion,' I said.

'I'm sorry,' said Socrates, 'I promised to take Xanthippe to the Gaiety to see *Mrs Miniver*. I shall be in trouble if I'm late.'

'I've got some prep,' said Francis and, throwing his towel over his shoulder, walked quickly over the meadow towards Bishop's Hull.

The sun was setting, and a cold breeze was getting up. The single garment which Socrates wore winter and summer flapped gently against his hairy legs. We stood silently watching the small impudent figure, which had now broken into a run, its white shirt conspicuous against the dark hedgerow.

A quest for philosophy which, like this one, takes the form of composing a 'Quest for Philosophy,' might reasonably begin as we have begun, with a dialogue, in which thoughts are shown issuing from a thinker. To the philosopher in whom philosophy is still fermenting the form of dialogue will always be attractive, for in such a person a conflict of thoughts is a conflict of possible ways of being himself.

If it is the philosopher's duty to question everything, this initial dialogue might well be devoted, as ours has been, to a question about questions. But it may seem strange that we have not asked, still less answered, what seems to be the obvious question about questions: What is a Question? But here we have a regress, though not a vicious one perhaps: to ask that is to ask a question, so presupposes at least some form of knowledge of what a question is. And such knowledge as it does presuppose is quite enough for our present purposes. But if someone were not content with that reply he could cause us serious difficulties. He would be asking us for a definition. And people who ask for definitions of terms in common use are almost always laying traps (if they are not laying traps, they are just wasting breath). They want to make some sort of capital out of the reply, either by showing that it leaves out something that they want included or that it includes something they want left out. Unless one knows in advance what the trap is, one cannot frame a reply that will avoid it: demands for such definitions are, in fact, riddles. But to show good will, I will provide two definitions of questions. A semantic definition of spoken questions: utterances whose purport is not that the utterer knows something and wants to impart it or wishes something done and requires to have it done but that he doesn't know or understand something and wants to be informed or to have it explained. That definition is fuller of snags than a dune is of rabbits, a real trap-setters' paradise. A syntactic definition of written questions: any form of words that if correctly translated into English would probably be terminated by '?' rather than any other mark of punctuation. Let the standard of propriety here be the practice of a professionally-trained member of the editorial staff of a major publishing house. This definition also is full of glorious loopholes (supposing editors disagree? just imagine!), and could almost certainly be shown to be inconsistent with the other: in fact, one of the old jokes mentioned in 'Franciscus' turned on the fact that 'I want to know the time' would be a question on one definition but not on the other. But what this shows is not that correct definition is a very tricky business demanding great gifts of intellect, but that the enterprise of defining degenerates into a silly parlour game unless carried out in the context of some real and specific difficulty that needs to be cleared up.

Questions appear in 'Franciscus' in three guises. First there are riddles, questions purely external and detached from any personal predicament. Next there are the questions implied in the interchanges of the dialogue, in which each person questions the others by way of finding out what sort of people they are and answers by way of revealing his own self to them. Thirdly there is philosophy, the mode of questioning that they end by discussing and that the whole dialogue discusses, a mode whose status as riddle or confession, as exercise or way of life, is problematical.

What the next two essays explore is this problematical status. For we already saw in our introduction that the philosopher's questions have this dual context, the context of his own life and that of the philosophical activity as such. And each of these contexts may be seen in two ways. They are the settings that provide meaning, that give philosophical questioning its point. But they are also the sources of error. One enemy of truth is private bias; the other enemy is professional bias. Philosophy is a habit of questioning. The very habit of asking and answering questions affects the substance of our thinking; and the form and context of the questions asked determine what kinds of answer will be accepted. But, at the same time, the kinds of questions that I can take seriously, and the kinds of answer to them that I can offer and accept, will depend on the sort of person I am.

In 'Credo ut Intelligam' the necessity of the personal context is proclaimed; but it is shown that truth depends on the negation of the personal context. Then in 'Is Reality Really Real?' an attempt is made to cut out personality by exploiting an impersonal technique; but the result of the enquiry is an impersonal demonstration that lack of personal context entails falsification, and a hint that the more impersonal the technique the more arbitrary its use.

The basic problem of communication and understanding is that I remain I and you remain you; but, if we did not remain invincibly ourselves, there would be nothing to impart and nothing to understand. No philosopher between Plato and Jaspers really took this situation seriously. How this situation works itself out in an academic context is what we now consider.

Credo ut Intelligam

*Credidi, ideoque intellexi appears to me the dictate
equally of Philosophy and Religion.*

S. T. COLERIDGE

The academic lecture is a strange institution. As a way of transmitting
information it is, in the age of the printed book, absurdly inefficient;
as a means of provoking thought it is so ineffectual, when compared
with the challenges of seminar and tutorial, as barely to merit the
name of 'teaching'. Yet in many subjects at many universities no
instruction other than lectures is offered. So it is not surprising
that those in this odd trade should often be asked, and often ask
themselves, what they are up to. Some, no doubt—those leaders of
thought who feel able to do some of their leading from the lectern—
feel no unease and should feel none. But in any university the mass
of the teaching personnel (no other term seems appropriate) lack
that standing. I am concerned for that majority whom a stern
curriculum requires to lecture annually for forty years on Plato or
Herbert Spencer. If they are neither provoking thought nor imparting
indispensable knowledge, whatever can they be doing? Surely a
practice so common must have *some* excuse.

Well, what do we do when we lecture? Some of us, having made
beforehand notes of what we think should be said about what, use
these notes only as insurance and control; in the lecture hall we
compose our souls to silence and allow whatever may be in them to
well forth—not 'We lecture' but 'It lectures in us', as Lichtenberg
nearly said. Obviously, this is not the only method. There are tales
of yellowed and brittle pages read verbatim from generation to
generation. And our method is plainly an unreliable one, for the
mental wells may run dry, or become muddied, and whatever truth
may be in them will then have a hard time to scramble out, and its

features when it comes will be neither attractive nor easy to discern. Surely, one thinks, any lecturer expounding an author should be able to state what he said, explain what his words meant, elucidate references to thinkers and events of his day, and point out the fallacies in his arguments as he states them, all in an orderly and systematic fashion. That, it seems, is what some of our colleagues manage to do, and it is clear that many students prefer such a performance to what they get from us. But to me at least this method is not open. I cannot bring myself to say in the lecture hall anything whose truth does not at the moment seem to me a matter of interest and possible concern.

The odd method I have been describing, and the odd reluctance on which it rests, are not beyond explanation. They imply a definite view of the nature of philosophic truth; and those who think that they are simply wrong might ask themselves whether their objections and demands are not themselves based on a particular view of the nature and communicability of truth. Our practice is justified if in philosophizing the philosopher's whole mind is expressed and his whole personality involved. His ideas and the truth which he believes are his truth and ideas, and no one else's. For example: if I believe, and manage to get you to believe, that truth is in this way personal, my belief and yours are different beliefs. They differ not in the trivial sense that you and I are different persons, nor in the outrageous sense that our beliefs have nothing at all in common, but in the limited though important sense that in each of us the belief in question is one of many beliefs and attitudes which do not sit side by side in mutual isolation but exist only as a compound, the nature of each component of which is conditioned by the rest and by the whole. Thus a belief by which I live can be ignored by you, although you share it, because in you it has no context that makes it effective. It is indeed very common for one person to say something to another with passionate conviction, only to receive the reply 'Of course—what of it?'

The cohesion of beliefs makes communication of fundamental opinions and attitudes a very slow and uncertain task. It was for this reason, perhaps among others, that Plato (or his ghost) refused to make in writing a formal and literal statement of his deepest convictions, although he said (in his Seventh Letter, 342 c) that it could be done easily and briefly. For they could not be effectively transmitted without living together, the student working alongside the teacher until he assimilated from him the validating context. So living, the student would at last see the truth 'in a flash', for it was a very simple truth whose significance was all in the possibilities of its application. It is also because Plato knew that our minds work in this way that in the imaginary city of his *Republic* everyone is to be taught to believe the 'myth' of the four metals. The perfect city cannot thrive unless all acquiesce in certain simple truths. But the uneducated populace lack the intellectual depth in which these truths could take root: the mental context which alone could give them meaning does not exist and could not practicably be imparted. The myth then acts as a fruit, bearing with it its own context as a pulp to sustain its kernel. Only, since the masses are trained to have fine feelings but not fine minds, the context that the myth supplies is not an intellectual one, but emotional.

All histories and text-books of philosophy, however many their epigrams, are fundamentally dull. What they offer is a no-man's idea: statements of supposed fact which anyone may accept as true or reject as false as he pleases. I never yet heard of anyone being persuaded to accept an author's views by what a textbook tells of them. It is quite a different matter when we turn to his own writings. Here we meet what alone in philosophy has value: the person thinking, the lived idea. Only at this stage can we make out the possibilities of an idea as a living force to be seized or abhorred, made one's own as a positive or a negative influence. And our chances of making such real use of what we read are greatly increased by what we can discover of the writer's life and times.

If histories and textbooks are as dead as they have just been made out to be, are we to attribute their prevalence to wickedness and perversity in those who compile and use them? We are not. The demand for slogans and summary conclusions which they meet may be regrettable, but is inevitable. In acquiring the full understanding of which I have spoken one must start somewhere and follow some route, and neither starting-points nor way-stations need resemble destinations. One must have something to use as a focus or a nucleus for one's thoughts. And the need is especially obvious in an unfamiliar subject, where one's scattered thoughts must be brought from a distance. First steps are bound to be dull, and textbooks bore in a good cause.

Slogans and summaries serve as mnemonics. That is their true function, and as such even the most earnest thinkers use them. The trouble is that, since they are thoughts symbolizing (even if also stimulating) thoughts, they may come to be mistaken for the thoughts they symbolize. In the case of such a thinker as Thales, where the symbol alone survives, we are victims of a misfortune without remedy; but we have ourselves to blame if we let the slogan stand as conclusion for a thinker whose works are preserved. Textbooks, by their very nature, tend to commit just this fault and to encourage it in others. If my estimate of the nature of philosophical truth is correct, the complacency with which many teachers of philosophy allow such textbook learning to occupy their minds is astonishing and disgusting.

From one who would lecture on a philosopher and avoid the textbook's error, one may ask two things. First, by scholarship and imagination he should re-build his author and present his thoughts as the author would himself have done had he been addressing foreigners of time and place, explaining what they meant to him in his own day among his own people and why it seemed necessary to say just that just then. Then the lecturer should present the ruminations to which his author's words provoke him in his own actual environment. The former process is necessary to preserve and convey the unique flavour of the presented fact; the latter is necessary because the fact presented is so strange. For the communicated idea requires two contexts. There is the context which it had in its author, but which he neglected to make explicit because his contemporaries necessarily had it from their own experience. This the lecturer recreates and attempts to convey. But his students, who lack some of his years and learning, cannot receive this context effectively: they cannot overnight transform themselves in imagination into Athenian ephebes or Parisian schoolmen. Except for brief flashes of insight, then, the ideas must remain dead for the student unless he can be shown them at work in a context with which he is already at home. So the ideal lecturer will for half his time hide behind his subject, and for the other half obtrude himself. And all the while he presents the disconcerting spectacle of a man thinking. It is because this is thought to be a sight worth seeing that lectures are still given. And the more a lecture resembles a talking book the less it shows of the thinking man.

Some students may well prefer talking books to thinking people. A talking book is more purely useful to the prospective examinee, for a thinking person must be treated as an end in himself and not merely as a means to an end. His humanity gets in the way. And for the same purpose a real book may be even better than a talking book, except that the latter may have been more recently revised. So one speaks of *reading* for an examination. One may get a very good degree without ever having heard a thought fired in anger.

Books are almost always better organised and more concentrated than lectures. One may consult them at one's leisure, and re-read the difficult bits. It really is not surprising that serious students prefer reading to hearing. Just so, many people would rather listen to a phonograph record than go to a concert. The recorded performance is almost sure to be a fine one, and concerts are chancy affairs: indeed, being edited to flawlessness from snipped tapes, the recording will be freer from lapses and errors than even a very good live performance. And one can play it at leisure and repeat it at will. One wonders why people ever attend concerts. But the answer is simple. For one thing, even today, the sound has to be trimmed down before it can be got into the box. But far more important is that a live performance is live, a concert is a real happening with real people in it and a proper beginning and ending. The phonograph record is nothing but the notes. Just so, a man's thought must be cropped before it will fit between covers. The tone of voice has to go, the gestures are discarded, nothing is left but the words. But far more important is that in a book nothing real is happening, whereas even in the most grindingly dull lecture a real person is really up there droning away to a genuine human slumberer or two. So people keep on going to concerts and lectures, even if they are not very good. Going to a lecture or a concert is doing something, while reading a book or listening to a recording is not doing anything, but just profitably filling in time.

The philosophers about whom we lecture were thinking men themselves. As with any man, the better we come to know them, the less we care whether they were right or wrong. An expert can go through a work by Aristotle, for example, chapter by chapter, demolishing each of his propositions as mistaken, incoherent, misstated or invalid, and end by reaffirming the supreme worth of Aristotle as a philosopher. His opinions are assigned a value that does not depend on their truth or untruth, and this is not merely his skill in perpetrating fallacies that point towards subtle and important truths, nor his usefulness in providing opportunities for versatility in rebuttal: it is the sheer human worth of a man delicately and passionately thinking just so. Such a delight in the factuality of fact is, naturally, neither shared nor appreciated by most students, for theirs must be a textbook knowledge. They do not dwell on, and scarcely recognize, the fact of the man thinking, and press straight on to the blunt question: is he right or wrong? For, if he is wrong, they do not see why they should bother with him.

It would be wrong to imply that the students' question is out of place, or shows immaturity or vulgarity. To be as indifferent to truth as the connoisseur of philosophies whom I have described is to be a dilettante, and a paid expounder is scarcely justified in indulging in such an attitude in business hours. So some kind of answer must be given. But the question turns out to be not quite so simple as it may sound. For the statements of which it is asked may be value judgements, and the philosopher may have been quite right to formulate in his place and time an evaluation which it would be quite wrong for us to make in our own. And he may have been quite right to draw certain conclusions from certain beliefs which he had good reason to think true but we have better reason to think false. But let us suppose that the question is one of fact, and that what we are asked is: Is this true, or is it not? And let us suppose that we do not call a statement true just because it follows logically from a system of beliefs that its author happens to hold, unless we have sufficient reason to think that he rightly held them—that we refuse to call it 'True for the Kwakiutl and false for the Navajo' if it happens that the former believe it and the latter do not. Then, so long as its reference is unambiguous and sufficiently precise, the truth or untruth of the statement will not depend on its context of belief in author or reader but only on its relation to some state of affairs to which it refers; and we will be able to say confidently that it is either definitely true or definitely false, however hard it may be to find out which it is.

If that is what the students are asking, it is not unreasonable of them to expect a downright answer, even if the answer be only a confession of ignorance. But now it appears that what can be true or false is not the lived idea, mine or yours, but a no-man's idea, one abstracted from these and considered in abstraction; for its truth is not to depend on its membership in this or that set of lived beliefs. This abstracted idea, which of course is what textbooks and textbook-style lectures traffic in, is much easier to handle. It is held in common: if my belief is true, then your belief, if it would normally be called the same, is also true. Such beliefs can be readily passed on, without loss, from person to person. But we must remember that this abstraction, this no-man's belief to which alone the concepts of truth and untruth can be directly and strictly applied, is neither my belief nor yours as we hold them and live by them. It is for this reason that the category of truth-or-untruth seems inadequate for religious beliefs and other kinds of belief that tend to be passionately held and to be 'hard to put into words'. In such beliefs, what is most immediately important is just their relation to the lives of their holders, just the part they play in the economy of an individual mind; and that, of course, is what the question of truth leaves out of account, just as the pawnbroker ignores the 'sentimental' value of the trinkets put before him. It would be helpful in heated discussions if disputants could bear in mind that what is true or false is not the idea as it is believed in, but the lifeless doctrine that can be abstracted from it.

Scientific theories cannot be believed in the same way that religious beliefs are held, without ceasing to be science. The possibility of science depends upon its propositions being treated as abstractions. The propositions which go to form a scientific theory do indeed depend upon a context, but in a different mode: they take their meaning and importance from the theory of which they form part, but the theory itself is supposed to be public in the sense that it means the same to all who understand it. Only while it is being formed or challenged is a scientific theory a matter of vital concern, when it is contaminated with the emotional attachments of those who labour to establish or destroy. And at such times it may become unusually hard to discern just what a theory asserts or denies. It may be that without an intensity of involvement that makes the risk of such confusions inevitable no one would care enough about the sciences to keep them going. But that belongs to another enquiry.

Augustine said that faith in religion must precede understanding: if one does not believe, one cannot understand. To many this seems obscurantism of the worst, a shameless attempt to evade the duties of explicitness and rationality, allowing the theologian to say whatever he pleases without heed to any objections save the superficial ones of other theologians as deeply prejudiced as himself. To others, what Augustine says seems obvious truth, borne out by their own finding: he is not claiming a privilege, but stating a truth about the working of the mind. It is possible, say Augustine's friends, that his opponents take him to mean by 'belief' a purely intellectual assent, as to a demonstration in geometry. But the faith of which he speaks is not this: he describes it as a trust, a confidence as in a person's word. The 'I believe in' of a creed is not the 'I believe that' of an opinion. We are not asked to assent to propositions that we do not comprehend, but to forget about propositions altogether until we have experienced for ourselves the kind of living to which they refer. Now, if the argument about beliefs that I have put forward is sound, Augustine's demand is justified. The affirmation of a theologian will then serve less to persuade, convince or instruct than to articulate an attitude already held. And certainly we may allow Augustine this much truth: that believers talking of religion with unbelievers often feel that they are discussing different things. But if theologians have been misunderstood by unbelievers who subject them to inappropriate criticism, they are themselves to blame; for they often insist that what they say is true. And we have seen that what is true is an abstraction. Insofar as what a theologian says is meant to be true, it is open to the same public discussion and criticism as any common coin of discussion; insofar as it claims exemption from such criticism as the symbol of a rich inner experience, the category of truth or untruth is inappropriate to it and there is nothing in it for the unbeliever to unbelieve.

Does Augustine's thesis hold for philosophy as it does for theology? If it is true that philosophy proceeds from the whole man, then it seems to follow that the thesis must hold, that commitment to a philosophy is necessary to its understanding. And it is certainly true that most professional philosophers have succeeded in understanding only what they believe. But one had taken that for mere weakness. If it is no weakness, but the inescapable condition of the philosophizing mind, it seems that there can be no rational comparison or choice between philosophies: the way in which one philosophizes is to be explained only by the mysterious workings of conditioning, reaction and conversion. Well, it may be so. But it need not be so. Faith is not the only theological virtue: there is also love. Just as one does not need actually to become another person in order to understand how he feels, but by sympathy may imagine oneself in his shoes, so there seems no reason why one should need to make an intellectual position one's own before one can understand it, so long as one can sympathetically abandon oneself to it in imagination. Large phrases like 'Philosophy proceeds from the whole man' may mislead; what the argument demanded was not that one must be wholly committed to the truth of every philosophical proposition that one effectively entertains, but that philosophical propositions make effective sense only in connection with each other and only from the standpoint of a believer. But there is no reason why such a standpoint should not be taken up out of sympathy and provisionally, by a person of supple mind and good will.

To adapt another of Augustine's sayings: *Dilige et quod vis dic*, love and say what you like. No doubt something of the position thus sympathetically taken up will remain as a permanent part of one's own thinking and thus impair one's bigotry, just as a person given to sympathy may find it hard to relapse into pure selfishness. But this risk is probably already inherent in understanding itself.

Augustine may still have been right about theology. No doubt to a theologian all opinions but one are heretical, and it must be wrong to sympathize with heresy, so that it may even be sinful to understand a theological position other than one's own. But that is a question for theologians to decide.

There is still a third theological virtue: hope. While we are at it, can we find a place for hope in the strategy of philosophical understanding? Indeed we can: without hope one would never embark on the long task of understanding at all. There is both the plain sort of hope, that the effort to understand will be rewarded by something worth having given one's mind to, and the more subtle hope of which Gabriel Marcel speaks which is akin to faith but less determinate, being no more than the refusal to believe that apparent nonsense is as nonsensical as it looks. So now abideth faith, hope, love, these three; but the most significant of these for the philosophical understanding is love.

In my youth I was nurtured by a school of analytical philosophy whose twin breasts may be seen, in the light of the present argument, to have been giving milk of quite different colours. By taking one side or the other, one would err by attending exclusively to the private or the public aspect of thought. On one side were G. E. Moore and his followers, who seemed never to deal with actual thinking but only with the textbook abstraction: they ignored what people meant and dissected what their words seemed to say. Their work thus failed to be (what some of them claimed it to be) the whole of philosophy. It did not, in fact, come to grips with philosophy at all, but only with what textbooks make philosophy out to be. It therefore had a great vogue among those who were able to confine their knowledge of the attacked philosophies within those limits. Ranged against them were a mysterious and perhaps quite imaginary band called 'therapeutic positivists', who refused to consider ideas at all outside of their personal context. The philosopher was to remove the muddles of an individual's confused thinking, by talking to him and letting him talk until he realized that there was really nothing for him to be puzzled about. Such philosophers thought it proper to undertake the cure or conversion of only one puzzled person at a time, and for preference one whom they knew well. They would not admit that their nostrums had any common curative property. And that surely was wrong of them. Logical refutations may be valid, and common confusions may be demonstrated. Surely there is a place for refutation and demonstration. And on professional philosophers (a type of being on whose peculiarities it may be that these therapists had not sufficiently reflected) their emotional impact is often considerable. After all, the ideals of lucidity and rationality are not so esoteric as to defy exposition, nor so private that they can be pursued only on the couch or in the confessional.

Both wings of the analytic movement (if I may thus vary its anatomy; and there was always something sphinxlike about it) shared the belief that when verbal tangles and their consequences had been cleared away whatever might be left was no concern of the philosopher. They differed in that the Mooreans thought that the tangles always existed in isolation, the therapists that it was virtually impossible ever to isolate them. Both were mistaken, alike in what united them and in what divided them. Although the tangles do not exist in isolation, they can be abstracted and treatment prescribed for them; and some people can dose themselves. Then, when the tangles are cleared up, one must look at the context from which they were abstracted and see what is left. What we may find, my argument has suggested. Whether we shall like what we find is another question.

One could state the present condition of our search for philosophy thus: that in 'Credo ut Intelligam' we have argued for what 'Franciscus' presented, a philosophy that is the outward form of the man thinking, that is the expression of a whole personality. But the argument has also shown that such a philosophy eschews truth. And this will hardly do; a philosophy that indulges self-expression at the expense of veracity is a betrayal of all that western thought has won from myth and fantasy. We therefore turn to the opposite extreme, to a philosophy that disavows personal involvement or even personal interest in favour of the deployment of a technique. Of the two modes of analytical philosophy caricatured at the end of 'Credo ut Intelligam', one was exploited in 'Franciscus,' and the other now engages us: we turn from the excessive particularity of the mutual therapy of engaged and mutually bemused individuals to the abstraction of the purposeless operation of analytical procedures in vacuo.

Even if it had not meant giving truth up, the idea of a philosophy that expresses the whole personality of the philosopher is an absurd one. A man's personality is not the sort of totality that can find such expression: his personality is variously active in all that he says and does, and any such sample of his words and deeds as his philosophy may comprise could never be more than a representative selection. And surely every philosophy, as every deed, must represent or express the agent's personality just because it is his; beyond that, it is ludicrous to suppose that an 'existential' philosophy is more characteristic of its author than a formalistic philosophy is of its author. To say that a philosopher's work expresses his personality can mean only three things. One, that the philosopher means what he says; but any philosophy may be sincerely meant, and sincerity can scarcely be verified anyway. Next, that his everyday concerns spill over into his philosophy; but one sees no value in that, since if they are irrelevant they will merely distract and if they are relevant we need not enquire into their biographical connections. Third, that he never changes his mind. This is true of many philosophers, but hardly to be counted in their favour. It seems to follow that a personal philosophy is simply a bad philosophy, preferred doubtless by some as more 'human' and comfortable, but by the same token less demanding, less genuine, less philosophical.

'Franciscus' in fact, despite the apparently existential fusion of personality and thoughts, stressed the author's detachment no less than 'Is Reality Really Real?' does: the presupposition of a dialogue is precisely that its author does not mean what is said, that the ideas it holds are worthy of attention but not of belief. Unless one is in two minds one cannot write in two characters.

'Franciscus' explored the form of philosophical discourse, 'Credo ut Intelligam' the activity of philosophizing. It remains to introduce into our discourse the object of philosophy; for, after all, whatever the philosopher says, he must say about something. And what could this be but reality? It seems inevitable that the next move in our quest should be to consider the nature of reality; or rather, in the recursive mode that is already becoming obviously the characteristic manner (if not mannerism) of this enquiry, to consider what it is to consider the nature of reality. And this is precisely what we are going to do. The question posed is one of those off-beat questions discussed in 'Franciscus'—Francis' fourth type. It looks, in fact, like a riddle of the eighth type. But it is treated as if it were a serious request for something, if only we could find out what was wanted. Since the investigator is also the propounder of the question, the pretence cannot be taken seriously. But, as we have just seen, both the question and the solution offered acquire, as it were, a posthumous significance from their transference to the context of this book. The piece ends, in fact, by considering the relation between what a philosopher says and what there is for him to say and for him to say it about; and in the two essays that follow the precise significance of this very problem turns out to provide the object of our whole inquiry.

Is Reality
Really Real?

What a question! It seems obvious that the answer must be 'Yes,'
for if reality is not real it is hardly likely that anything else will be.
But, at the same time, the question seems to have no definite meaning. If somebody asked you this question and you assured him that
reality *was* real and he then asked you to give your reasons, could
you be sure that the reasons you gave would be of the kind he
wanted? Besides, the answer is no less obviously 'no' than it is 'yes.'
For, although if whiteness is not white it is hardly likely that anything else will be, it is equally true that whiteness can never be
white. Only white things are white; whiteness, the abstract quality
of such things, can never be. If whiteness were white it might be
painted some other colour, and then where would we all be? Similarly, we might say, only real things are real, and reality can never
be. But really, now, is that really obvious?

If our question has no definite meaning, perhaps we can give it
one. Perhaps it is like that other baffling question, 'What is life?'
That is a question that is often asked by people who are genuinely
puzzled; only, they are not all puzzled about the same thing. Thus
we can say that the question has no definite meaning, but is lent a
meaning for the occasion by people who ask it. What that meaning is, one can usually find from the context: either it will be
embedded in a discussion which will fix the meaning, or the person
who asked it can be called on to explain what he wants to know.
But if there is no context there is nothing to discuss: one can at best
give a philosophical meta-reply, which might have two parts. The
first part might classify the different sorts of things that the ques-

tion might reasonably be used to mean; the second might discuss why anyone should think that such a question could be answered as straightforwardly as 'What is the date?'

A few years back, meta-replies of the second sort were a recognized genre of philosophical writing: people were constantly discussing why people should be puzzled by meaningless questions, and suppose that they had simple answers. But the fashion has rather died out, partly because it was increasingly recognized that the questions that really puzzled people were by no means meaningless in context, and partly because it is only too easy to understand how a philosophically unsophisticated person may come to think that what he means by such a question is what the question itself means. In any case, the genre is closed to me. So far as I am aware, no one has ever expressed any puzzlement through the form of words, 'Is reality really real?' It would not be profitable to discuss why someone might think this was a proper question with a discoverable answer, when no one in fact thinks so. Nor can I derive a meaning for the question from its context, since it has no context but stands isolated at the head of a page. And there is no questioner to interrogate but myself, who cannot explain what I want to know when I ask the question because there is nothing particular that I want to know. I do not myself think there is a problem about whether reality is really real, and if there were a problem I do not know what it would be, nor whether I should find it puzzling or interesting. Finally, it would be absurd to classify the different real questions that might lurk under this one form of words, since so far as I know nothing in fact lurks there. Whatever I do cannot start from any real predicaments but must begin, at least, as a sterile manipulation of verbal symbols.

Since our question has no standard interpretation or set of interpretations and no context, it begins to look as if it may be incurably meaningless. But it need not be so. Granted that the exact import of a question will always depend on the unique living context in which it is asked, what it means can usually be inferred from the meanings of the words in it. Otherwise, dictionaries would be useless. But this inference becomes harder, the more the context of the word varies from those in which the word usually figures, and if the context is too odd interpretation becomes quite impossible. If I am told that 'The tunq-bird has a scarlet head,' I have received information, because, although I do not know what tunq-birds are like otherwise, I know where birds wear their heads and I know what sort of colour scarlet is: as soon as I see a tunq-bird I shall know whether I have been told right or wrong. But if I am told that 'The tunq-bird is lazy' I have learned nothing definite. I don't know what laziness in birds is. Does it consist of (for example) making all movements in a desultory manner, or sleeping long hours, or hanging around the nest while the female tunq-bird goes out to forage, or all or none of these? But I do know that the laziness of the tunq-bird must be something of this kind, some of the many possible modes of avian behaviour that are analogous to what would be laziness in a man. If my informant was a truthful man I shall expect, when I have the chance to watch a tunq-bird in action, to be able to recognize for myself what he meant by calling it lazy; though if he was a liar I shall never know just what lie he was telling. Thus, when I was told that the bird was lazy, although I learned nothing definite, I was given a pointer towards learning, perhaps even a blank that would become learning when properly filled in. If, on the other hand, I were told that 'The Absolute is lazy,' that would convey nothing to me at all. I should not know whether it was a slangy reference to the 'principle of cosmic laziness,' or a complaint that the concept of the Absolute did no work in metaphysical theories and could be done without, or whether perhaps 'The Absolute' was not the name of a racehorse. I should just have to wait for more light. The difficulty is not that I am faced with a mere succession of marks or noises that I am trying to pretend make up a sentence, nor that there are too many possible meanings to choose from, nor that the sentence is too vague. The difficulty is that I know perfectly well what sort of thing 'The Absolute' means, and what *sort* of quality 'lazy' stands for, and all that I know suggests that the two expressions do not go together. Lazy is not the sort of thing that the Absolute can be, and the Absolute is not the sort of thing that can be lazy. Thus, if the sentence is to be fitted on the procrustean bed of sense, one end must be taken as standard and the other end hacked about to fit. A new meaning must be found either for 'the Absolute' or for 'lazy.' But which end should we hack? And how should we hack it? As things stand, the decision is entirely arbitrary, and the whole procedure consequently irrational. Of course, if the sentence were used for communication, the context would tell us what to do: even metaphysicians, however careless about verification, are usually scrupulous about 'logical grammar,' as these considerations of the mutual adaptation of concepts are sometimes called.

But, lacking such context, we can do nothing but sit and wait with folded hands.

Now, how stands our question about reality? Its case seems less hopeless than that of the lazy absolute, for two reasons. In the first place, although reality isn't the sort of thing that we usually call real, it isn't the sort of thing that we feel can't be either real or unreal, either. In the second place, we can easily see which end to start hacking: from the look of the words alone, the meaning of 'reality' should depend on that of the more basic word 'real', rather than the other way round. So perhaps we can do something to find a meaning for our question, or at least a plausible range of meanings that it might have.

Finding meanings for meaningless sentences is hardly standard procedure. But I have precedents. I have heard reputable philosophers say that, although they didn't want to say that God's existence (supposing God to exist) was not necessary, they didn't know what would be meant by saying that it *was* necessary, and it was time they (or someone) found out. Their attitude might seem to justify F. H. Bradley in calling metaphysics 'the finding of bad reasons for what we believe upon instinct.'[1] But they had excuses. They wished to square the claims of personal piety with those of professional honesty, and they wanted to harness a powerful linguistic habit to an intellectual engine. Besides, they suspected that there might in fact turn out to be sound philosophical reasons for saying that if God exists he necessarily exists—after all, even if one claims not to know what either sentence means, one can scarcely deny that 'God exists and necessarily so' has a much more plausible ring than 'God exists, but might not have'—and, if so, it should be possible to work out what the reasons are. Besides, God's existence was first said to be 'necessary' for what seemed at the time to be cogent philosophical reasons; but now, perhaps because we are more sophisticated, the reasons no longer carry conviction and the conclusion is left to dangle. I do not have any of these excuses. I am not tied to any position on whether reality is real, let alone whether it is really real, by any ties of piety, or linguistic habit, or professional scruple, or respect for tradition. I am impelled by nothing more than curiosity to see what happens. If I were asked where this is getting us I should have to reply that it is getting us nowhere, that philosophy's task is not to get anyone anywhere, not even itself, but to stay in its comfortable bed, just bouncing up and down to test the springs. And this I take to be the meaning of those who say that philosophy's whole task is analysis. . . . Analysis! the very word is like a bell.

Let us then test our springs. If I can give an account of what 'real' means that is both flexible enough to cover all or most of its usual uses and also definite enough to survive transplantation to the indeterminate context of our invented question, I shall be able to give the whole question meaning by working out senses for 'really' and 'reality' on the basis of that provided for 'real,' and mechanically combining the results. If not, I must leave the question meaningless, for the alternative is to assign it some meaning arbitrarily, and for such an arbitrary meaning any other collection of unassigned vocables would have done as well or better.

But just what is it that I am trying to do? Am I inventing a meaning for our question, or discovering one? If I am inventing, what prevents me from just inventing as I please without more ado? But if I am discovering, is it not strange that I can find in my own utterance a sense that I did not know was there? Fortunately, I need not choose either interpretation of my undertaking: I can say instead that I am *constructing* a meaning, or *developing* one. Really I am in no different case from any philosophical analyst since Plato's day. All philosophers who perform analyses of concepts are trying to sell their public something, even if they are themselves their own first and best customers. Uses and meanings revealed in analysis are isolated only by the analytical procedure itself: previously, there was just the word with all its uses. If all philosophy is analysis all philosophy is a fiddle, though good philosophy is a crafty fiddle. Of course, words are used as they are used, and the philosopher has to follow along; but the explanations that he gives are not produced by the phenomena that they illuminate, and very different interpretations of the same phenomena may shed enough light to pass muster. Every philosopher is the inventor of what he says, even if not of what he says it about. However, since I have no axe to grind, and since I would rather pose here as discoverer than as inventor, I shall not produce an analysis of my own, but shall garble some of the work of other thinkers and try to establish a modus vivendi among them. No doubt I shall come up with something.

The modern cult of analysis starts with G. E. Moore. Let us begin at the beginning. F. H. Bradley had claimed in his *Appearance and Reality* that time was unreal. Moore complained that Bradley had no business to use the word 'real' and its derivates in this connection unless he meant *at least* what ordinary people meant by the word—

if he meant something else, he should have said something else.[2] In common speech, according to Moore, 'is real' usually means no more than 'is'; and the rest of the argument is devoted to showing, with his usual painstaking subtlety, that 'time exists but is unreal' is self-contradictory. But does anyone really mean 'is' or 'exists' by 'is real'? That people sometimes think they mean it is shown by the rhyme about the faith-healer of Deal, who said that, though he was certain that pain isn't real, when he sat on a pin and it punctured his skin he disliked what he fancied he felt; but the same rhyme also shows that in fact people who think pain unreal admit that something exists that they dislike. The opposite of real silk, as J. L. Austin said, is not non-existent silk, but imitation or artificial silk; and the opposite of a real pain is not a nonexistent pain but an imaginary or hallucinatory one, or even a very slight one. By analogy, one would suppose that if Bradley meant by 'unreal' what people usually mean by it, in saying that time was unreal he would be saying not that temporal phenomena don't exist but that, though they exist all right, they are hallucinatory or nugatory or—something. What, then, had got into Moore's head? I was at a loss to explain, until I chanced upon the 1887 edition (the fourth) of *A Vocabulary of Philosophy*, by Wm. Fleming, D.D., wherein I read: 'Real, the. The existent (1) as opposed to the non-existent . . . . Green maintains that the real consists in relations.' There were five other things that the real, the existent, could be opposed to; but the first was the one that struck me. If this was how philosophers wrote when Moore was fourteen, an impressionable age, we can forgive him much. But what he was defending in the name of common speech, and using as a stick to beat Bradley, was nothing but a philosophers' barbarism now happily obsolete. Perhaps what enabled him to persist in his error was the supposition that because a real lion, as opposed to an imaginary lion, is one that exists as opposed to one that doesn't, 'Unicorns are real' is an acceptable way of saying that there are such things as unicorns and 'Unicorns are unreal' would be a normal way of saying that there were no such things. Now, people do say all sorts of odd things, but I am not sure that I have ever heard 'real' used thus, and I am quite sure that I have never heard 'unreal' used so; and what is more, the *Oxford English Dictionary* hasn't either.

It is useless for me to defend 'ordinary language' against Moore's onslaughts unless I am prepared to explain how the word in question is actually used. In the present context, it seems suitable to begin by amplifying the conjecture we have already made and asking how

Bradley uses it. Oddly enough, Moore seems not to have thought this question worth asking; and in this neglect he is imitated by Lazerowitz, who follows Moore unquestioningly both in equating 'is real' with 'exists' and in ignoring what Bradley actually says, thus providing a ready-made solution to an imaginary problem.[3]

Bradley says what he means by 'real,' but his account is neither clear nor consonant with his own actual usage. There are times when he slips into Moore's error of equating 'exists' with 'is real,' and further complicates the issue by his belief that 'What is real is the individual';[4] but he has an official doctrine, and in the passages that Moore is attacking he sticks to it. This official doctrine is that what is unreal is self-contradictory, and what is real is self-consistent. The doctrine seems both extravagant and paradoxical: surely it is to objects, events and so on that the terms 'real' and 'unreal' are usually applied, whereas it is creeds, propositions and so forth that are called self-consistent or self-contradictory. Granted, a man may be called consistent if his deeds or utterances are all of a piece, but one would not convey that by calling him 'real.' However, the paradoxical doctrine is arrived at in a quite straightforward way, as follows. The account of some relation given by philosophers is found to involve self-contradiction; it is claimed that the relation in question can be thought of in no other way; and the relation itself is then said to be self-contradictory and hence unreal. Apart from the verbal equation of 'unreal' and 'self-contradictory,' then, we have the doctrine that a thing is unreal if the idea of it is self-contradictory. Let us look a little more closely at how this works out in *Appearance and Reality*.

Bradley says that his task is to criticize 'the ideas by which we try to understand the universe' (page 11); he speaks of finding 'a way of thinking about facts in general which is free from contradictions' (page 120) and of examining 'some ways of regarding reality' (page 241). Thus he sets up the scaffolding of his argument in terms of 'ideas,' 'ways of thinking,' 'ways of regarding reality' and the like, of all of which it is certainly appropriate to ask whether they are consistent. He fills out this framework with a general attack on the idea of 'a relation,' and particular attacks on the ideas of particular relations. Since, as we have seen, 'Green maintains that the real consists in relations,' he is thus attacking at least some philosophers' notions of 'the real.' Now, among the particular relations that Bradley impugns are temporal relations, and it is thus that he falls foul of Moore. He argues that a duration cannot be composed of instants having no duration, any more than a line can be made up of points having no extension, and with this one might agree. But he goes on to say that 'such ways of understanding are forced on us by the Nature of the Universe' (page 307), and here I cannot follow him. Why should the universe be blamed for filling people's heads with foolish notions? Certainly there have been philosophers who felt obliged to think thus,[5] but I should rather ascribe their sense of obligation to their own intellectual bent than to any remoter cause. Other philosophers, such as Aristotle and myself, feel no such duty to commit nonsense. Only solid bits of stuff, we should say, can be broken down into or built up out of smaller bits; time, not being a chunk of gunk, cannot be composed of anything. No doubt some people do have self-contradictory notions about time; but that is no reason for saying that there can be no consistent idea of time —of duration and succession, of recollection and foresight, and whatever else we may gather together under the head of 'temporal phenomena'. Let us suppose, though, that in fact no single coherent account of all such phenomena could be formulated. I do not see how this could really be so, but, if it were, it would certainly be a reason for saying that time was unreal, that what we all thought we meant by 'time' was something we couldn't possibly mean because it made no sense. Bradley's error lies only in saying that this is proved to be so by the currency among some philosophers of one particular set of incoherent notions; and in then going on to suppose that because an idea is self-contradictory it can properly be called 'unreal,' and because a thing is unreal it may be called 'self-contradictory.' He slips into saying such things gradually, and apparently unawares. Although, as I said, the framework of his discussions is set up in terms of ideas and ways of thinking, the discussions themselves are carried through in terms of what the ideas stand for and the thoughts are about, and this change of level seems to escape his notice. Thus it is that reality and consistency come to be equated. We can see Bradley starting down the slope when he writes (page 76) 'Anything the meaning of which is inconsistent and unintelligible is appearance, and not reality.' For surely terms, and not things, have meanings; but things, and not terms, constitute reality.

So much for how Bradley thinks he uses the term 'real.' How does he actually use it? We saw that reality is ascribed to whatever can be consistently thought about. Unhappily, Bradley is so beguiled by his fusion of reality with consistency that he never comes closer to a reasonable account of his own usage and procedure than a complaint (page 399) that in a certain context 'Neither the subject nor the predicate possesses really the nature assigned to it.' If a thing does not have the nature assigned to it by our thinking, then, it is not real; if it cannot have it, it cannot be real. But for an adequate formulation of this usage we must turn to a later Warden of Bradley's college, G. R. G. Mure, who defines the real as 'that which actually does possess the nature which it claims, or which is claimed on behalf of it.'[6] This definition, which corresponds to the *Oxford English Dictionary*'s A.3, shows just what Bradley means when he denies that time is real. If this definition be accepted, the discovery that ideas about time that everybody held were self-contradictory would justify one in saying that time was not real, since it could not possibly 'possess the nature' which everybody 'claimed on behalf of it.' And the definition also gives a fair account of how the word 'real' is ordinarily used, as we shall now see.

Mure writes as if the two halves of the disjunction that his definition presents were different ways of saying the same thing, one perhaps more metaphorical than the other. But in fact they correspond respectively to the adjectival and predicative uses of the term. 'Is this a real diamond?' might be paraphrased by 'Does this possess the nature which we claim on its behalf *by calling it a diamond?*' 'Can this be real?', as in the mouth of one who doubts whether he wakes, is better represented by 'Can this possess the nature which it claims?' Let us enlarge on this distinction.

The adjectival use of 'real,' besides being irrelevant to our present concerns (for we asked whether reality was real, not whether it was a real somewhat), seems relatively free from problems, although philosophers have spent most of their time on it. In all such contrasts as those of real silk with imitation silk, real trains with toy trains, real beer with ginger beer, and the like, the suitability of the suggested paraphrase seems so plain as to need no further comment. I shall only add that 'real' comes inevitably to be used as a synonym of 'perfect' or 'good'. A perfect so-and-so, like a real so-and-so, is one that possesses to the full the 'nature' that the use of the term 'so-and-so' implies. The only difference is that in the 'perfect' thing no part is defective, nothing is missing, broken, inadequate, substandard, immature or decayed; whereas in calling a thing a 'real' somewhat we think not of the parts but of the whole, for which nothing is substituted and which is in no way phony. A perfect such-and-such must be a real such-and-such, but the reverse entailment does not hold. Similarly, if I was right in holding that someone who calls a thing a 'good' somewhat may be taken as saying that it is such as to satisfy 'the' wants of 'the' persons concerned with somewhats, it is plain that only real somewhats can be called good somewhats, but 'good' may convey more than 'real.'[7] But because one way of being phony is to be substandard, 'real' may sometimes be used to convey the full force of 'good' or 'perfect.' If you saw a particularly splendid sunset you might say 'Now, there's a real sunset for you,' meaning thereby that everything people ask of sunsets and mean by 'sunset' was exemplified therein. It is this use of 'real' that I once saw exemplified by price-labels in a shoe-store window, as follows: 'Value, £1/-/-'; 'Good Value, £1/10/-'; 'Excellent Value, £2/-/-'; 'Real Value, £2/10/-.' Mure's definition fits such usages excellently: instead of saying 'There's a real sunset for you' (or 'That's *something like* a sunset!') one may say 'That's what I call a sunset'—with its disparaging converse. 'I don't call *that* a sunset.'

The best-known contemporary discussion of the word 'real' is that of the late J. L. Austin, to which I have already alluded:[8] it covers the adjectival use only, and may seem to run counter to what I have said. Pointing out that the opposite of a real train is not an unreal or non-existent train but (for example) a toy train, one may then go on to say, first, that 'real' has meaning only by contrast with such terms as 'toy,' 'imitation,' etc.; second, that since these contrasts differ widely, 'real' has no unitary meaning of its own; and third, that the expression 'a real X' has a definite meaning only where some such expression as 'an imitation X' is current.[9] In saying positively and generally what is meant by calling a thing a real somewhat I fall foul of all three of these assertions. But one could reply to all three that there is a difference between the meaning of a locution and the point of uttering it on any occasion or type of occasion. Certainly one would have no occasion to talk about real X's if there were no toy X's, imitation X's, fake X's, and so forth, and if no one dreamed or hallucinated X's; but that would not invalidate our account of what the locution would mean if it came to be used. Again, the point of saying 'It wasn't a real snake' is quite different as directed to the victim of a practical joke (it was only a piece of rope), a sufferer from hallucination (it isn't really there, none of the rest of us can see it), or a zoological tyro (it was a legless lizard); but the meaning of the statement can still quite fairly be said to be that the snake failed in some way (unspecified, but not needing to be specified) to fulfil the specifications of a proper snake. It is quite true that the term 'real' does not stand for any set of recognizable characteristics, such that a man who knows nothing about X's could recognize a real one, as a man who knows nothing about tunq-birds can recognize a red one. Accordingly, if 'the meaning of a word' were 'the method of the verification' of its applicability, we should have to say that 'real' meant many things since there were many routines for verifying whether it was applicable, the appropriate routine not even being always the same for any given X. But I should state quite flatly that that is not what 'meaning' means: it is rather the epitome of a highly controversial and obscure theory about the conditions of the intelligibility of statements. I should insist that 'real' has a single meaning in so far as a single account of what it means can be given that will hold for all its various applications.

We saw that the laudatory exclamation 'That's a real sunset' can be idiomatically replaced by 'That's what I call a sunset.' So it might be suggested that calling things real has more to do with how things are described than with the things themselves. Thus, instead of saying 'Is this a real so-and-so?' one might ask 'Is the term "so-and-so" correctly used to describe this?'[10] To say that this is after all what is meant by calling things real so-and-so's differs from the account we have extracted from Mure (that what is meant is that they possess the nature we claim for them by calling them so-and-so's) only in its implication that the question is not one about the thing at all but about the term. This would be fair enough, reminding us that realness is not a quality like squashiness, were it not perhaps even more important to remember that the man who wants to know whether he is being served real coffee or that powdered muck is worried about what he is drinking, not about what he is saying. And of course this account of what talk about real things actually means fails altogether to cope with the predicative use of the word. Perhaps we can say that 'This is a real X' means ' "X" is correctly used to describe this'; but in 'This is real' there is no word 'X'. It is one of the great advantages of Mure's formula that it can be jiggled, as we have jiggled it, to cover the predicative use as well: 'This possesses the nature which it claims.'

The predicative use of 'real,' like that of most adjectives, is relatively rare; and it is about this use alone that problems arise. Consider the phrase 'Life is real' (earnest, too). Moore seems to think that this would mean 'There is such a thing as life,' as we see by substituting 'life' for 'time' in his thesis against Bradley: 'What more, we might ask, can a man who says that Time *is* real mean to maintain about it than that it exists, is a fact, and is? All that most people would mean by saying that Time is real could, it would seem, be expressed by saying "There is such a thing as Time." '[11] The substitution makes the absurdity plain. Mure's version would be: 'Life possesses the nature which it claims.' But what would that mean? To speak of things claiming is to use an animistic metaphor: surely things don't claim anything, only people claim things for them, as we suggested before. But the metaphor is not pointless. Things do something like claiming, in that people often do feel that certain ways of thinking and speaking about things are forced on them by experience—a feeling that we have seen Bradley shared, and that is expressed in the common phrase 'I can't help thinking. . . .' The world into which we are 'thrown' is not a mere surrounding to which we are indifferent, as though we were statues on a junk pile: it is a world organized, as Heidegger has eloquently explained, into systems defined by active relations, as it were into tool-kits;[12] and in these relations things variously importune us as potential agents. However, the animistic implications of the metaphor are not to be exploited here, and in some contexts we might prefer the theistic implications of an alternative metaphor, 'Is this thing what it's got up to look like?' Use of the word 'real' implies absence of phoniness and deception, but implies nothing about the possible source of the deceit.

What nature, then, does life claim? What is life got up to look like? What seems to be meant is that life is not hallucinatory, not a dream, not a texture of illusions; that the distinction between the 'world' of the imagination or daydreams and the world of 'real life' is a valid one. This meaning of 'real' is the one that comes closest to its root in the word *res*, 'thing': 'real' here means 'belonging to the order of *realia* or *things*,' and in this sense alone is negated by 'unreal.' The order of 'things,' the public, perceptible world in which we live, provides a standard of reference to which all dreams, pictures and imaginings are referred, and which all imitations imitate, and in it are found the 'natures' which they all 'claim.' Thus the 'real world' and 'real life' are not so much those which possess the natures which we claim for them by calling them 'world' and 'life' as those in which things are what they seem to be. But although 'Life is real' *seems* to mean that life is not a dream or anything like that, that cannot be what it really means, for it is nothing but the dullest of platitudes. *Of course* the distinctions between the imaginary and the given, between waking and dreaming, are valid. What is actually meant is rather that the claim of 'real life' to serve as a standard must be upheld: that waking does not stand to anything further as dreaming stands to waking ('And the world is not a dream'). And I suppose that 'Time is real' would usually mean that there is no standpoint from which temporal phenomena would be shown up as something like mere tricks of perspective.

Analytical philosophers used to be fond of quoting what children might say. It was felt that childish speech was free from self-deception; the fact that it abounds in naive error was overlooked. There was always the wild hope that if we all shouted 'The emperor has no clothes!' his pants would fall down. But they never did, and the fashion has rather died away. It is sad: there was something rather touching in that romantic yearning for a pre-philosophical innocence of language—'Unless ye become as little children, ye shall in no wise enter into the kingdom.' Anyway, as I was leaving a cinema one evening I heard a child ask: 'Mother, was it real?' Obviously the child's question didn't mean 'Did it exist, was it a fact, was it?' Of course it existed or there would have been nothing to ask about, and mother could not have known what 'it' referred to. What the child wanted to know was, precisely, were the things in the movie what they were got up to look like, did they possess the nature which they claimed, did what seemed to happen really happen, is the blonde really dead? Things are looking bright for the men from Merton.

Some would say that the distinction between predicative and adjectival uses that I have been relying on can and should be got rid of by saying that for 'is real' the words 'is a real (somewhat)' can always be substituted. 'The bear you saw last night was real'—a real what?—a real bear, of course. No doubt it would be hard to say what the somewhat would have been for the child at the cinema; but, after all, the 'it' in 'Was it real?' is not self-explanatory. One would have been justified in asking 'Was what real?' And then various substitutions might be used to represent the child's concern: Were the events in the film real?—real events? Or, was the lady's death real?—a real death? But of course one is not puzzled by what the child says, and can blithely answer: 'No, it was only a pretend.' For the 'it' is the film, surely, which although it is a real film, does not possess the nature which it claims, of being a slice of life caught in the camera, but is merely a mock-up.

Of course the 'real somewhat' trick can always be worked somehow, but, as in the case of the child at the cinema, it often needs a good deal of artificial and ad hoc supplementation. From 'Is reality really real?' we cannot continue 'Real what?—real reality.'

We would have to find something else to stand in for the 'somewhat'. That would be quite possible, as in the case of the child at the movies (who should have been in bed long ago), if we knew beforehand what the point of the question was: we should then know what sort of supplemental fakery to perform. As it is, we don't. In fact, the trick only works well in cases like that of the bear, where what is asked about is an individual, and the question is whether it is a real specimen of what we called it, whether it possesses the nature we claimed for it by calling it a bear. Perhaps we might restrict the predicative use of 'real' to such contexts, ruling out our own question (as well as 'life is real' and 'time is real') as an improperly framed expression. That would solve our problem for us, all right, and would leave the world a better and sweeter place; but it takes hardihood to stigmatize as improper forms of expression that are in quite common use, and the mood of this essay is too irenical for such nephelococcygian ukases. So I shall stick with Mure, suitably adjusted and expounded, and say that what we are asking is whether reality really possesses the nature that it claims. This possession of claimed nature, it seems, may come down to belonging to the waking world, being neither dream nor hallucination; etymologically, it suggests membership in the order of *res* or 'things.' To Bradley, it means being such that a self-consistent account of it is possible. When 'everything seems unreal' it seems not to possess the nature which it claims, is apparently not what it is got up to look like, seems not to belong to the waking world but is dreamlike or has a hallucinatory quality, seems to have no part in the world of things moving and being moved in public space but to be shadowy or a figment of a private fancy, is not self-consistent but is wavering or absurd, ungraspable.

We have now assigned to 'real' not a precise meaning but an area of meaning well enough marked out to be workable. It still seems likely that reality, whatever it turns out to be, will prove to be real. But is it *really* real? What does 'really' add? Not much. Sometimes it just gives emphasis: if I go out in the rain I get wet, if I fall in the lake I get really wet. So perhaps reality could be real but not really real, not so damned real as all that. Alternatively, one can say such things as that 'Canada is nominally a monarchy and apparently a democracy, but really it is superficially a bureaucracy and fundamentally a plutocracy.' The force of 'really' in such contexts is merely to acknowledge that some other opinion has been mooted. If reality had been supposed to be unreal or somehow bogus there would be some point in saying that it was, really, real. More usually, though, questions with 'really' in them question the truth of appearances and accepted doctrines. On the other interpretation, our question would have meant 'Granted, reality seems not to be real, but may it not perhaps be real after all?' On the present interpretation it means rather 'Granted, reality seems to be real; but is it really?' The only difference between the two versions is that one invites the answer 'Yes' and the other the answer 'No': in both cases the adverb invites the respondent to think carefully before replying, and not to be taken in by appearances either way. 'Really' in questions simply functions as a precautionary word, putting the respondent on his mettle. But I am on my mettle already. I shall be equally on my guard against being taken in by the apparent realness of reality and its apparent lack of realness, and I shall also be prepared to find that reality does not possess whatever nature it claims in so full a measure as it conceivably might. So that will do for 'really.'

Now that we have made one end of our question fast we may fix a meaning for the remainder, and thus for the whole, by hacking the other end about accordingly: that is, by establishing a meaning for 'reality' on the basis of that already established for 'real.' One might think this unnecessary, on the ground that 'reality' is a simple word whose meaning may be approached directly. But I do not think it is so. One uses the word confidently and unreflectingly in such phrases as 'in reality,' and in contrast to unreality and appearance, and thus supposes that what stands on the solid side of these contrasts is always the same. But there is no reason to suppose that it is so, and when we come to formulate just what it is that stands there we have nothing definite to guide us. Specific accounts of what reality is are all theories: the term 'reality' is not only theory-laden but theory-proclaiming. To accept any current account of what reality is would be to deliver ourselves into the hands of some theorist. And this I do not want to do, because whatever our question means I do not wish to reduce 'Is reality really real?' to a mere equivalent of 'Is so-and-so's account of reality really true?'

Unfortunately, it is also unclear just how a meaning for 'reality' is to be derived from what we said of 'real.' Various routes seem open. The most obvious is to take 'reality' simply as the abstract noun derived from 'real,' as equivalent to 'realness.' It then looks as if we have a question about the quality of realness, the quality that real things have in virtue of which we call them real. If we take it that way, reality cannot be real, cannot possess the nature which it claims, because we have sufficiently seen that there is no quality of realness, that we do not call things real in virtue of any shared characteristics. However, there is no call to take the word in just that way, for we have given no reason for thinking that all abstract nouns derived from adjectives function as labels for characteristics in any interesting sense. Thus, if 'reality' stands for whatever characteristics real things share, those characteristics might be no more than the fact that they qualify for the word 'real' to be applied to them. So we must look again. Let us clear the air first by substituting a less controversial term (say, 'heaviness') for 'reality,' and seeing how our question might then be taken.

'Is heaviness really real?', 'Does heaviness possess the nature which it claims?'—these equivalent questions may be taken in two different ways. In one way, we take them to ask whether the distinction between 'heavy' and 'light' is workable, whether we mean anything by 'heavy' definite enough that we can find experiential warrant to back our usage up. And it seems clear that we can. In the other way, we take the question to ask whether the heaviness that we admit to be actually detectable is what it seems to be: a quality in things pressing down, and so forth. And here the answer is no. We think that what we experience as heaviness is a phenomenon produced by the mutual gravitational attraction of bodies, and moreover that what we call heavy depends in a complex way on our expectations for particular classes of object as well as on the strength that our muscles happen to have. In this sense, heaviness is not real, inasmuch as by calling things heavy we imply that in themselves and apart from all observers they would still be heavy, and this we believe not to be the case.

The same two meanings may be found if we replace 'reality' where 'heaviness' stood. The first meaning is now: is the distinction between what is real and what is not real a workable one, can it be supported and demonstrated in actual cases? And here the answer seems to be that it can. The distinctions that we generally make in these terms, various as they are, generally work, and normal adults do not usually confuse, for example, the real with the imaginary. Making this more general, in accordance with our equation of real things that possess the nature which they claim with things belonging to the 'real world' of publicly accessible *res*, the question becomes whether the status of membership in the world of *res* can be successfully attributed to things. And again the answer is that it obviously can be and is: that in the contexts where questions such as 'Am I awake or dreaming?', 'Did it happen or did I imagine it?' and the like arise, they can very often be settled, and, where they cannot, it is easy to say what would settle them—the tracing of a putative witness, for example, or the discovery of physical traces or scars left by an event.

The alternative version of our question raises greater difficulties. Does this status of membership in the public world possess the nature which it claims? This question plainly differs in no significant way from the question whether that world itself possesses the nature it claims. Is the real world real, then?

What does the real world—the public world in which we waking move—claim? It claims nothing; it just sits there. Any 'claims' that it makes are made upon special sorts of people in special sorts of cases, who as we said can't help thinking that they 'can't help thinking' about the world in some special way or other. But if that is true perhaps we can turn the truth around and say that the claim to be evaluated is that the real world makes no claims but just sits there.

Does the real world, then, possess the status of an objective world, independent of all observers? Centuries of philosophical endeavour have made plain the many ways in which it does not: colours and sounds exist only for viewers and hearers, duration only for rememberers—and so on endlessly; we cannot here recapitulate the whole of western metaphysics. The 'public' world, to be public, must be accessible to observation, a world as observed. The status of independent world is that of a world as unobserved, a status held only by a system of entities with which we have no acquaintance, combined in relations of which we are unaware: a world that really makes no claims whatever.

We may next ask, as an alternative version of our question, whether the public world in which we waking move possesses the status of a public world. The waking world, as opposed to the 'worlds' of our dreams and daydreams, is the same for all, and is always the same for each one of us in the sense that our observations and recollections of it are reliably linked. But if we ask ourselves whether this public world is really public, we see at once that of course it is not. Just as the only world independent of observation would be an unobserved world, so the only world independent of individual interpretation would be an uninterpreted world. But the 'real world' for me is the city I live in and the people I live among, and what makes these the real world for me is the way they cohere as my environment. And the manner of this coherence is determined by the organization of my interests, which is not the same as yours. Heidegger and *Sartre* have exhaustively shown how each of us lives in a world of his own, and how the idea of a world itself depends on the cohesion introduced and imposed by the consciousness for which it is a world; and again I do not propose to repeat their demonstrations. I will only emphasize that it is *my environment as I know it* that claims to be a public and 'real' world, and that this claim certainly cannot be sustained.

This argument, however, cannot be allowed to stand without its reversal. The way in which I share with other people my responses, my enjoyments and repugnancies, restores inexpugnably the primitive conviction that we share a world. What you point out to me, I can see; we should be as cautious of making too much as of making too little of the fact that my cerebral cortex and yours are two cortices and not one. By sufficient abstraction it may be made to seem doubtful that my experience and yours are alike enough that the world of our environments could be called the same: what I feel when in pain might be utterly unlike what you feel; the colour I see as red you may see as green or as some colour altogether outside my experience: so long as each of us discerns a difference whenever the other does, such qualitative unlikenesses could never be detected. But concretely this is not really plausible; the texture of our agreements and disagreements, sympathies and antipathies, is so subtle and close that we cannot really convince ourselves that your world and mine have any other differences than we can account for by the differences in our habitat and the describable differences in our physical and mental constitution. Thus, if the real world 'claims' to be public in the sense that it is as much the same for me and you as a view is the same for my right eye and my left, the claim must be disallowed; if the claim is only that I can recognize a place from your description, it must be allowed; and, since all this talk of 'claims' is metaphorical, there is nothing to make us accept any one version of what 'claim' may be being made rather than any other.

Another claim that we make for the real world by calling it a world is precisely that it is a world, that is, a totality of somewhats whose membership is determinate. Or, lest it be said that our emphasis on the word 'world' is factitious here, we may say that by speaking of 'reality' in this sense we do imply that some things are part of 'reality' and some are not, and we should be able to say which they are. But which? Fish, rocks and airplanes, obviously yes.

Shadows? They are publicly observable, though not solid, and they can be definitely located. Rainbows? They are observable, but not solid, and can only be located angularly, from a particular viewpoint. Desires and feelings? They are not publicly observable, but a person without them would not be a real person. Dreams? They are the paradigms of what may be contrasted with reality, but dreamers really have them and are affected by them. Do we wish to confine 'reality' to the world of sense experience? or to the world of solid things ('material objects')? or to the sum of things that must be taken account of (and by whom)? None of these alternatives is free from familiar difficulties. Is the world of sense experience made up of colours and sounds, and so on, or of coloured and noisy and stinking things? Can I see you or only the colours of your surface? If you hurt yourself, can I witness your distress? On the second alternative, are people with their personal characteristics 'material objects'? Are electrons? Is materiality to be defined in terms of the domain of some science or sciences, or in terms of the way in which things enter into our experience? And on the last alternative, is there anything that may *not* need to be taken account of by someone at some time? So long as such questions can be raised, the idea of reality as a single world or order with determinable constituents seems not merely nebulous but utterly misleading.

Is it possible to say what lies behind this elusive idea of a 'real world,' an idea that in so many contexts is so easily workable but that seems to resist formulation in any general terms? William James said that 'Reality, howsoever remote, is always defined as a terminus within the general possibilities of experience.'[13] When we have winnowed away the chaff of illusion and appearance, we are left with the grain of reality. The question before us is whether there is any one winnowing process, whether all lines lead to the same terminus. Toulmin has persuasively argued that what we call 'reality' is always, precisely, the terminus on some particular line of enquiry, that of which some specific interest must take account: the scientist's 'reality' is not the artist's 'reality.'[14] If so, it would always be a mistake to think of our experience as being capable of being split up into discrete 'levels,' of which some one could be taken as the top, or bottom, or anyway ultimate, level. And if that is a mistake, no candidate for the status of terminus can succeed, not because there may always be something beyond the supposed terminus but because no candidate has the unity requisite to constitute a 'level' or 'order' of experience.

From the same lectures whence I gleaned the equation of 'This a real X' with '"X" may properly be used to designate this' I also derived the thesis that the fallacious supposition that reality is a single graspable notion is the basis of metaphysics; and it may well be the case that metaphysics has in fact proceeded on the assumption that experience can be stratified and the strata then graded. Even G. E. Moore, who attacks Bradley's handling of this grading, seems to concede the underlying assumption, for he writes: 'Reality may be spiritual, for all I know; and I devoutly hope it is.'[15] To deny that reality is really real would then be to deny that metaphysics of the traditional sort is otherwise possible than by singling out one line of enquiry as paramount and its terminus as a terminus terminorum. Since I do not wish to embark on the rather large task of investigating what could possibly justify or invalidate such selection, I pass over this interpretation of our question with just one remark: though the supposition that such an enquiry (an enquiry, in effect into the possibility of integrating all possible interests and enquiries in some fashion or other) *must* succeed is doubtless fallacious, and the supposition that the enquiry can be effectively carried out may well be mistaken, the question of what the conditions are in which such an enquiry could be pursued, and its possible procedures specified, and of whether those conditions actually obtain, seems to be one that may reasonably be posed. And if so, though a dogmatic metaphysics may be a wild-goose chase, a problematic metaphysics is not; although it may, of course, not promise to repay the effort.

Even if the more ambitious and far-reaching (and interesting) stratifications of experience fall victim to the suspicions just voiced, one sort of stratification seems likely to survive. We are all familiar with the experience of waking from a dream, and no difficulty that we may experience in cataloguing the latter will reasonably inhibit us from contrasting as a whole the many worlds of our dreams with the one world that we know when awake. On waking we discover, or decide, that the world of our dream does not possess the nature that it claimed, that of providing an enduring environment for our endeavours and, more relevantly for our present interests, of being a world from which there is no awaking. But then, if the world of our waking, viewed in the same way as an interwoven mass of experience whose constituents need not be precisely catalogued, should prove to stand to some further order of experience as dreaming stands to waking, we shall have to say that the world of waking does not possess the nature which it claims, either. And so on. But the series 'as dreaming is to waking, so waking is to X, and X is to Y . . .' must stop somewhere. The fraudulence of each state is discovered in its successor, but there must be a last stage in the series that has no successor and so is never found out. In fact, it seems to possess the nature which it claims, and we shall call it 'reality.' From this standpoint, there are at least three questions that 'Is reality really real?' might ask. One is: Is the waking world (or some other purported terminus) the real terminus? This seems to be an intelligible question. Many people are prepared to say that in some moods they find the world 'dreamlike' or 'hallucinatory'; one can readily imagine waking from life as from a long dream. But the question seems not to be even in principle decidable. It is only by comparison with the coherence and continuity of waking reality that dreamers know they have been dreaming. Even if a dreamer feels sure that he is dreaming, he cannot establish the fact otherwise than by waking up. So one can see no reason to suppose that any context of experience into which one 'awoke' could be *known* to be such that no further 'awakening' was possible, since it is part of the very notion of a 'waking' state that in it the convictions of the relative 'dream' state are discovered to be illusory. (Conversely, one is not justified in dismissing one's convictions or those of others as 'illusory,' or in indulging in any form of scepticism, in the absence of the more comprehensive framework that a waking state supplies: the mere hypothesis that there may or must be such a state is not sufficient.) Secondly, then, our question may be taken to mean: is there such a series of states, each of which is 'waking' and/or 'dreaming' to another? And to this we may surely say that there is indeed. The only possibility that could modify our experience of awakening in this regard would be that on death (for example) we should 'awake' into a dream from which we 'awoke' into an ordinary waking day, thus establishing a circle. But even this seems not to be a real possibility, inasmuch as what establishes a dream as such is its happening to a sleeping man who wakes before as well as after and in the meantime may be observed by others to be asleep. And lastly our question may be taken to mean: given the two levels of dreaming and waking, do we have them the right way round? or more generally, given any such series that may be held to have been validly constructed, can we tell which is the right end? The question appears to be no more than a vapid conundrum: unless some verbal trick or paradox is involved, there is no real question that the criteria of coherence, continuity and inclusiveness whereby we distinguish dreams from waking admit of no reversal. Our dreams do not envelop our waking lives. Still the word 'real' carries, as we noted, a certain prestige, and a paradox-monger might find the status of 'reality' worth fighting for, on behalf of some favoured mode of experience. But I do not think it worth while to conjecture what paradoxes he might choose to deploy, and to what end.

Thus far, we have constructed meanings for 'reality' on the basis of the predicative rather than the adjectival use of 'real.' But, as we remarked, the adjectival use is commoner as well as easier to explicate, and might have provided a better base. Our question would then become, 'Is the realness of real things really real?'; or, 'Do real things possess the nature which we claim for them by calling them real things (of the kind in question)?' For example, does real silk possess the nature that we claim for it in calling it real silk? And to that the obvious answer is yes, since the expression 'real silk' can be meaningfully and correctly applied. This answer has no interesting consequences at all. It might be thought to mark out a privileged realm of 'real' things, undisappointing, genuine and sound, as opposed to the realm or realms of the imaginary, shadowy, ersatz, imitation, pretend, toy, apparent, disappointing, half-hearted, and so on. But it does not. There is no such privileged realm, because anything whatever may appropriately be termed in some contexts a 'real' somewhat, even if only a real disappointment or a real fraud. A real cow, granted, is not a pantomime cow. But a real pantomime cow is not a hallucinatory pantomime cow; and a real hallucinatory pantomime cow is not a spurious one invented by a malingerer for the M.O.'s benefit. And so we might progress through dreams and mirages and fictions until we tired. But, it will be said, at the other end of this series stands the cow. Since we can knock no more words off, we may feel like saying that there is nothing more real than a cow. In the analogy 'real hallucinatory pantomime cow stands to real pantomime cow, as real pantomime cow stands to real cow, as real cow stands to X,' the last place cannot be filled. And yet an ordinary cow is not a real pantomime cow, though it may look like one and be used for one in country districts. In the series real pantomime cow—makeshift pantomime cow—hallucinatory makeshift pantomime cow—and so forth, the ordinary 'real' cow is in effect relegated to second place. What comes first in the series, and what order the other terms follow in, depends not on the nature of things but on what we are talking about and what we are saying about it. Still one might say 'They couldn't get a proper pantomime cow, so they had to use a real cow instead'—it would be more usual to say 'ordinary cow,' 'ordinary' being as derogatory as 'real' is honorific, but 'real cow' is perfectly intelligible in the context—so that one of the things that 'reality' might mean would be 'the totality of things which possess the nature which we claim for them by applying atomic nouns to them.' And perhaps it is to this totality, rather than those elusive 'worlds' of 'material objects' or 'perceptible reality,' that the notion of an order of *res* or 'things' is most apt.

By applying atomic nouns to some things and not to others we seem to set the former up as a privileged class: to sneer at the pantomime cow while we pin a medal on *bos taurus*. To ask whether reality is really real then becomes equivalent to asking whether this discrimination is justified: whether our distribution of atomic nouns is based on a sound judgment or is just a matter of linguistic habit; and, if the former, whether the soundness of our judgment rests on a sound assessment of our own personal and social needs or whether it rests on a fair recognition of the articulation of the world on and in which we pass this system of judgements. And this position may be generalized. In asking whether real things possess the nature that we claim for them by calling them real (whatever it is that we do call them) we may be asking, not so much about the implications of the term 'real' and the atomicity of the nomenclature that most often goes therewith, but more generally about the adequacy of nomenclature to what it names, and of descriptions to what they describe. We have already seen reason to say that 'real' and 'reality' are used with reference not so much to what things are as to what we say about them. And what this implies may be seen even in two usages that seem at first to tell against us: the equations of 'reality' with 'the facts,' and of 'the real' with 'the existent.'

'Common sense openly revolts against the idea of a fact which is not a reality,' writes Bradley in *Appearance and Reality* (page 423). 'The facts' are usually thought of as being inescapably 'there,' 'given,' the raw material one has to take account of, not affected by how one thinks about them. But what actually passes under the name of 'fact' is usually something rather different. Facts are what can be stated and marshalled: the facts of a situation are those factors in it that can be argued about in general terms. A person who tells another to 'face the facts' or 'face up to reality' takes himself, and expects to be taken, as telling his victim to come to terms with his situation as it really is; but what these injunctions amount to in practice is a demand that the victim think solely in terms of what can be made a matter of public debate. To decide wisely about one's own affairs one has to be swayed largely by what cannot be stated in this way. To acquiesce in the insidious demand to face the facts (or reality) is to agree to surrender all the niceties of one's own understanding and accept the simplifications of the ignorant: to forget, for example, one's intimate sympathy with and understanding of an individual, and replace it by 'the fact that' he is a negro, or thief, or belongs in some other crudely defined category. It is foolish, of course, to ignore 'the facts' altogether, for conventional judgements are important; but it is much more foolish to attend to nothing else.

Like the equation of 'reality' with 'the facts' is that of 'the real' with 'the existent.' 'The existent,' one would have thought, would likewise be what is unavoidably 'there' or 'given,' what one stubs one's mind on. And perhaps that is what we do try to mean by the expression; but it is doubtful whether we succeed. We have been taught by Russell to think of questions about existence as asking whether anything can be found to answer to a given description. If that is correct, the existent can be no more than the describable. It is, indeed, obviously true that we can only *affirm* the existence of something we can either describe or recognizably designate, whether through words or through some other form of symbolism. It is certainly possible to point to an Assyrian carving or a Cretan gem and say 'Did such things ever exist?'; but in so far as we confine ourselves to words (as we usually do) our questions about existence will be, not indeed about language, but about things only in so far as they can be described in our language. Thus when William James writes 'Anything is real of which we find ourselves obliged to take account in any way'[16] he means, among other things, that the real is what is really 'there' and so on; but 'accounts' consist of words, and one can take 'account' of something only so far as it can be stated as a fact. With such considerations in mind, we may be patient when we read in Reichenbach the truly grotesque statement that 'When we say "The bear you saw last night was real," this must be interpreted as meaning "The statement 'There was a bear which you saw last night' holds within the ordinary language"'[17]—as opposed, that is, to the dream language or the film language. One naturally resists this fomulation, even if one accepts the odd notion of what constitutes a 'language,' on the ground that one wishes to talk about bears and things, not about words at all. But the exaggeration that pretends that we are talking about words may help us to avoid the error of thinking that in discussing reality

and real things we are discussing things as they are all by themselves, and not things as our thoughts and words represent them.—
And of course even 'things' may let us down: we tend to acknowledge as a 'thing' only what is isolated by a definite description.
From all of this we may conclude that 'reality,' 'the real' in the
sense toward which our argument has been tending, is a sort of
shadow 'world' corresponding to the content of the infinitely many
things that may truly be said in whatever language we may be
using. I do not mean to suggest that 'the facts' are whatever we say
they are, or are brought into being by our stating them; only that
'the facts' as we know them and report them are formulated in
terms that our language provides. Even an expression that refers
without describing refers to its object under some designation and
hence under some aspect. It is of reality conceived in such terms
that I wish to ask whether it is really real, whether it actually possesses the nature that we claim for it by calling it whatever we call
it. And it seems that our answer might be either 'yes' or 'no.' It is
as though we were to ask whether a certain painting had the
properties ascribed to it in a postcard reproduction. An obvious
answer would be 'no,' on the ground that (for example) the postcard suggested that the painting was composed of dots, and elimi-
nated many subtleties of form, thus making out the picture to be
simpler than it really is, besides actually misrepresenting the colour.
But an equally obvious answer would be 'yes,' on the ground that
the postcard uses a familiar technique of reproduction and has
familiar limitations, and everyone knows that these are to be dis-
counted. There is nothing in the postcard to show which aspects of
it are to be taken as veridical, and to what extent—in fact, there is
nothing in the postcard to show that it is a reproduction at all. If
we take it as a reproduction we do so because of our knowledge of
reproductive techniques and practices; and knowledge of just the
same kind will show us how it is to be taken, will prevent us from
supposing that its original is dotted and from trusting the colours
in the same way that we trust the outlines. Whether we answer the
question by 'yes' or 'no' will depend on what we think the chances
actually are of people being misled. And the same is no doubt true
of our question about 'reality': whether we think that language is
misleading will depend on what we think the chances are of people
being misled, and on whether we think the ways in which they are
likely to be led astray are more important than the ways in which
they are not.

Within the area now marked out for our question, several possibilities remain. Here is one of them. If to ask whether a thing is a real X is to ask whether it possesses the nature which we claim for it by calling it an X, this might be taken as asking whether it conforms in every respect to the definition of X. To take it so would be to assume that for every term there is only one correct definition, but this is an assumption that has often been made. Reality could then be be thought of as the 'world' comprising all things-which-are-as-defined. That would give us a world that we glanced at before: the world of Platonic Forms, one corresponding to every atomic noun (in our own language or in some perfect language), which are always precisely as defined and thus imperishable, unalterable, and in no way imperfect or unsatisfactory. Is that world really real? Well, what is the nature which it claims? Its least claim would be to be a really existing world, independent of any other world or of what anyone may happen to think or say. That claim is generally disallowed; the reasons for making it are held to be reasons for thinking something quite different. Indeed, it is no longer thought worth discussing as a serious possibility. *A fortiori*, one rejects the further claim that the world of Forms made on Plato, to be a 'terminus within the limits of experience,' a world we might at last wake up to. Unless we are to undertake a monstrous task of rehabilitation, we shall have to agree that reality is not real at all, if that is what it and its realness are. An alternative claim would be that, for example, the 'Form' of cow corresponded to what was most cowlike in cows, that successful definitions correspond to things in their truest and most inward nature. But since the definition of 'cow' is unchanging (*ex hypothesi*) the 'Form' of cow does not change either; whereas a cow that is not constantly changing is not a cow at all. It is absurd to suppose that one can understand what cows are without reference to what cows do and what goes on in cows. Few memorable statements have been less helpful than Plato's dismissal of time as a 'sort of changeable image of eternity.' If that is reality and that its claim, it again does not possess the nature which it claims and is not real at all, let alone really real. And of course the supposition itself that there is only one correct definition for any given term is one that few would make nowadays. We tend to think rather that, save in mathematics and other similarly specialized disciplines, terms may be variously defined and objects variously described for various purposes, and that it is the purpose in hand no less than the subject matter that determines the appropriateness of definitions and descriptions alike.

To make our question one about definitions, as I have just done, is to make it easy to answer but uninteresting, and to narrow its scope unduly. Our previous discussion prepared the way for a different question, one hard to formulate without a well-you-know-what-I-mean: can we equate the real with the given, with what is 'there'? In other words, do all our descriptions systematically distort the world they purport to describe? That this is a reasonable question to ask is suggested by a fact to which I have already referred: in deliberating what to do in a particular situation, it is not wise to rely on words alone. Discourse should be supplemented by lively reminiscence and anticipation, words and their associations should not be relied on at the expense of visual and other images of the actual people and places concerned; what we can articulate is no more important than our inarticulate feelings. If it is true that we do not rely for our knowledge exclusively on the describable aspects of what we are familiar with, presumably we cannot rely on the descriptions of others either. So we might be led to suppose that language in such cases tends to distort judgement, and that a similar distortion is involved in all descriptions because we necessarily present ourselves or our audience with what we can verbally extract from the situation: that is, with a schematization. In describing we interpret, and our interpretation depends not only on what the thing is but also on what we think of it. And, we might go on, descriptions purport to depend solely on the thing described. So descriptions are not what they purport to be, and reality tends not to be real. On reflection, however, we might deny this, or some of it. Descriptions do not mislead us in reaching decisions, because our interpretations are themselves a genuine element in the situation in which we have to decide. Certainly, no description contains 'the whole truth'; but it is only in law courts that any such absurd totality is claimed. Certainly, too, a description must select and interpret; but an impartial description makes only such selections and interpretations as all its hearers or readers would themselves make; and, since everyone expects a description to interpret, the fact that it does so deceives no one. Moreover, it is only in theory that our interpretations are separable from 'the given.' 'The given' is not given to anyone, and the process of abstracting it from our interpretations and expectations is purely imaginary. And if there can be no such thing as description without interpretation it cannot be literally true that interpretation distorts description, since there is nothing independent for interpretation to distort. The only valid discrimination would be between valid and invalid, relevant and irrelevant interpretations. So perhaps reality is real after all, so long as we do not force extravagant claims upon it. But before we allow ourselves to be convinced by this rejoinder we may consider four familiar ways in which descriptions are necessarily unsatisfactory.

First, in order to be of use, the words we use in descriptions have to fall short in definiteness. For example, in order to be small enough to be manageable our vocabulary for shapes and colours has to fall indefinitely short of the infinite variety of actual forms and tints. For some selected shades and shapes we can formulate precise terms, for example, 'jezzard green' or 'sphere of 1 cm. diameter,' but if we have too many such our vocabulary becomes unhandy, and for the most part we make do with such terms as 'greeny-brown' or 'cigar-shaped.' To achieve precision we have to go beyond the bounds of description, and invoke the resemblance of some particular familiar object. It is possible, of course, to describe shapes and colours precisely by specifying equations of curves and wave-lengths of light; but such descriptions can be made intelligible, if at all, only by producing the light, or drawing the curve, and seeing.

Besides being vague, words are not vivid as events are vivid. They cannot prepare us for what happens by conveying its immediate and actual shock. Not only do we find ourselves talking about the *sort of thing* when we really want to convey the *exactly what*, but we are never able to make others see what it is about what has happened that justifies our reaction to it. If they have not had like things happen to them, they must use their imaginations—that is, pretend to themselves that they have. If they are too dull of sympathy, or too conscientious with themselves, to make this pretence, there is nothing we can do for them or they for us. In some contexts this does not matter at all, in others it matters a lot. One who describes an experiment does not want to give his readers an idea of what it felt like to be performing the experiment, but to give an account detailed enough to enable his readers to decide whether the experiment was properly carried out, and to perform it themselves if they have a mind to. There is no difficulty in giving such a description, nor is it in any way unsatisfactory. But describing a musical performance is another matter. One can say what notes were played, and can say something in general or evocatively metaphorical terms about how they were played; and one can describe in a similarly general or evocative way one's own reactions. One cannot give a clear account of what went on without thus describing separately the sounds and one's own reactions to them. But this split corresponds to nothing in what seemed to be going on: it is part of 'the nature that it claims' that the music is stirring, affecting and so on. The clearer one's description, then, the less justice it will do to what it describes. It is likely, too, that the music will have made an overall impression that was felt as a unity and as unique. But it is obvious that descriptions cannot be made to cope with such unified over-all impressions. What was experienced as single has to be described piecemeal. We can do no more than say that such an impression was made, and bestow vague encomia on what made it. It is such discrepancies between what things are really like and what it makes sense to say about them that led Marcel to say that 'To think, to fomulate, and to judge is always to betray.'[18]

Lack of vividness in descriptions is as inevitable as we found lack of precision to be. A language that could handily make as many distinctions as there are differences between things themselves would be so complex that no one could remember it; and a language as vivid as the world would simply be the world over again. To be as lifelike as an elephant the word for an elephant would have to be an elephant, and that would make it quite useless. No more avoidable is the third shortcoming of description, which is that languages can only do their work by dealing with what things have in common and not with what makes them individuals. We may speak, certainly, of their 'uniqueness' and 'individuality,' but the fact of their being unique is what they have in common with other unique things, not what makes them unique. By exhaustive or evocative description any desired degree of sharpness can be reached, but serially and without the instant impact of the thing itself. Above all, any description, however sharp its focus, is logically applicable to any thing that fills its bill; but any thing, however exactly it resembles however many other things, is not the same thing as any of them, but the very thing that it is and no other.

Lack of precision, lack of vividness, lack of individuality—all of these merge into one another, and may be looked on as aspects of a single great difference in make-up between the real world and the 'world' that a language can present. A fourth facet of this difference, or a fourth way of regarding it, is as follows. In using, as we must, the same word for any one of a class of objects, we take no account of the difference made by the context in which each of those objects presents itself. Places with which one has grown familiar have associated with them a special feeling-tone which one can imagine to oneself and can recognize, but cannot describe at all. So at least I find, and I must suppose that others find the same. When one moves from one home, or country, or family, or job, to another, one breaks up not only one's old pattern of behaviour but one's pattern of feeling and perceiving. When, after a while, a new pattern forms, it consists very largely of old habits re-established; but not entirely. And when, later, one moves from one to another of these places or situations where such patterns have formed, one slips easily into the old pattern associated with it. These characteristic feeling-tones affect the attitude to, and the perception of, particular objects and kinds of objects, especially (for some reason) tastes and smells. If you have lived at different times for considerable periods in two different places, it is likely that a cup of tea (for example) in one will taste quite different from a cup of tea in the other—as different as the same colour seen through different-tinted glasses. No doubt this explains the complaint that husbands are traditionally alleged to make: that what their wives cook never tastes like what 'mother used to make.' On this showing, what the wives fail to provide is the context of the childhood home. One can indicate such differences; but one cannot describe them, since they necessarily depend on what is unique to a given context in the life of an individual. Yet they might be of great importance in coming to a wise decision. No aspect of life does more for happiness and misery than these habitual contexts in which everything is experienced. But, because they are indescribable, in 'facing the facts' or 'facing up to reality' one would be expected to ignore them completely.

You must think me very foolish to complain that descriptions necessarily distort the world in these four ways, when the whole argument depends on the impossibility of any other sort of description. It is not that any better sort of language is possible. To remove or alleviate the 'defects' complained of would make languages unintelligible. So what am I complaining about? Nothing could be sillier than a lamentation that words are words and not things. This objection would be valid, if I were indeed complaining or calling for action. But I am not. I simply point out that, since we all have to talk and think in words, it is as well to remind ourselves now and again of the ways in which such talking and thinking are likely to mislead us if we rely on them exclusively. Again, you might object that it makes sense to distinguish between satisfactory and unsatisfactory descriptions, but no sense to say that all descriptions are unsatisfactory. They cannot all be unsatisfactory as descriptions, for the best possible descriptions are descriptions as good as any description can possibly be. And it can hardly matter if they are unsatisfactory as something other than descriptions. But this objection is not so unanswerable as it sounds. Descriptions are unsatisfactory as ways of conveying what things are like—there are better ways. But this is supposed to be one of the things descriptions are for, and sometimes there is no other way available. People who are called upon to 'explain themselves,' to find words for their reasons for acting and reacting as they do, have every reason to wish to describe what must evade description. It is idle to think, as some philosophers have seemed to do, that such people will not feel frustrated if they can be got to realize that the difficulties which they feel are ineradicable: they do realize just that, and that is what distresses them.

We are now in a position to conclude that so long as we take 'Reality is really real' to mean 'The "world" of things-as-described really possesses the nature it claims, that is, is the world of things-as-they-are,' we must deny that reality is really real. Or, if you prefer: the real is rational, but the rational is not real. This is, I think curiously close to the point Bradley was making when he wrote on page 225 of *Appearance and Reality*: 'Reality is being in which there is no division of content from existence, no loosening of "what" from "that."' Bradley, however, used 'reality' to mean just the opposite of what I have been making it mean. He meant by it something like 'the world as we should have to describe it (which we can't) for it to possess the nature which we should be claiming for it by so describing it.' Whatever is describable turns out to be, not reality, but appearance. If the meaning I have given to 'reality' corresponds to what people usually seem to be talking about when they use the term, Bradley's meaning corresponds to what people try to mean by it. It is in Bradley's sense of 'reality' that reality is really real by definition.

I have now given our question several alternative meanings, with answers to suit, and expressed my preference for one of the meanings that yielded the answer 'No.' I might say in defence of my procedure that my discussion has been methodical and systematic, free alike from contradictions and from unexplained leaps. But I cannot pretend that it has been very satisfactory. For one thing, I have not shown that my method might not develop yet other possible meanings for 'reality', nor given any reason other than my own distastes and predilections for adopting one of the meanings I did enumerate and neglecting the rest. For another thing, the very fact I have been able to assign a number of different meanings to the word indicates that it has no potent 'logical grammar'—by which I mean only that it doesn't mean anything in particular to begin with, which after all was the fact that started us off on our enquiry. If, then, one is to use the term to any effect in a serious discussion, one must not only state just what one is meaning by it, far more precisely than I have here done, but also deploy it in a discussion long enough to acclimatize it in the reader's understanding. Long as it has been, the present paper is not long enough for that. These facts and practices, together with the eccentric wording of the question itself, must have lent an air of unreality to the whole discussion. But in spite of all the false starts, loose ends, and undistributed middles, we must leave it at that. Human kind, as that eminent Bradleian scholar T. S. Eliot has taught us, cannot bear very much reality.

*The essay just concluded responded to a double commitment.
Internally, as it made plain, it fulfilled a commitment to a problem
the lines of whose solution were not predetermined or even
foreseen. Externally, as was not said, it sprang from commitment
to discourse consecutively to a given audience on a given day.
Commitments of this latter kind, though common in the academic
trade, are hazardous if not heroic ventures: how can one so trust
in one's future self? How can one be sure that one will in fact find
that one has something to say—not something worth while,
necessarily, but something? If one thinks about it, that is a great
and fearful mystery. The existence of a discourse so doubly
committed to a problematical future thus raises by its very existence
the question whether such commitment to an undeterminate task
might not be what philosophy itself really is—or, at least, what it
is for one who makes such commitments in hope and terror. And
this is in fact the possibility that is put forward at the end of the
essay that follows, which consciously (even self-consciously)
proceeds from the same double commitment as its precursor.*

   *The means by which 'The Central Problem of Philosophy' reaches
the formulation of its possible task is the consideration, under
another form, of the general problem that the manipulations of
'Is Reality Really Real' turned out to have raised: what to do about
the general limitations on explanation imposed by the conditions of
viability in languages. It now appears that this problem, which
arose as it were accidentally, may be a crucial and pervasive one for
philosophy as a whole.*

We thus discover a double relation among the items in this collection (or moments in this sequence). Beside the dialectic of detachment and commitment already stressed there is a conscious unfolding in each of an unforeseen conclusion reached by its forerunner. Ever since Hegel, explorations of the patterns in which thought develops have been hampered by the insistence on reducing all such substantial and serendipitous unfoldings to the pattern of a self-subsuming alternation between paired poles. Not every expansion is a reaction. None the less, our own dialectic of abstraction and concreteness, of commitment and detachment, remains. But it must be confessed that, thus far at least, it has not worked. In our exploration of the relation between thought and thinker we have been unable to detach ourselves from detachment. One piece argued abstractly about concreteness, detachedly about commitment; one represented commitment without committing itself (for the character in 'Franciscus' who bears the author's name is not the 'I' of that dialogue, and neither of them is given the most telling lines); and the third took detachment itself as its option. In all of them, the personal context required to give the thought anchorage was absent or fictitious, rendering the outcome playful and frivolous. This remains true even if they all share an unstated context of self-questioning and self-discovery that bespeaks a sincere or even a desperate hunger for a personal salvation through justificatory works. By contrast, the next paper overtly claims and emphasizes the real context of a real person speaking of an actual concern on an actual occasion. Surely here we have commitment itself, pure and raw. What could be simpler and more direct than just laying oneself on the line, in the spirit of those evangelical missionaries who tell their sheep to stop resisting and just let the Lord Jesus take over?

The missionaries' advice is all very well, but of course for the uninstructed there really is no such simple performable act as giving up and letting the Lord Jesus take over. There is no identifiable hold to be relaxed. And so it is with the effort to make one's philosophy the vehicle of one's sincerity. How can any of one's acts or words be more one's own than any other? The plea for sincerity becomes a plea for artlessness, and the sign of artlessness is formlessness: and why should an uncontrolled and formless utterance be more one's own than a controlled and shaped one? May it not be in the very controlling and shaping that the nature and authority of the originating person appears?

One does see what is meant. A controlled utterance is contrived

and edited, an uncontrolled one may give its author away. But even
so there is no help for us here. Uncontrolled utterance is not within
the possible scope of our assumed philosophical earnestness. One
must produce a coherent paper, and to do that the revealed
or expressed self must be edited into tidiness. No less than in any
other form of literary production the speaker must fashion for
himself a persona whose concerns are deliberately channelled and
restricted, both in their substance and in the form of their
expression. Perhaps the concern of the discourse that follows is
even more fictitious than the unconcern of its precursors. Our case
seems hopeless. But it may be that our dialectic is really working
for us after all; for such a persona as is here presented may be
neither a lifeless image nor a bleeding torso, but a shape cut from
life, no less living for its formality. And we may find, as foretold in
the beginning, that our extremity is itself our salvation, that we
have here no dilemma but a situation that may itself be exploited
no less successfully than any other. That is in fact what 'Speculation
and Reflection' will suggest.

Of course, none of these complications that torment us arise
when one is simply dealing with a problem that one finds of interest.
One then just gets on with the job. That is no immediate help to us,
for the presupposition of all this book is that it is not now clear
what job is to be got on with. But in the long run it may turn out
that nothing is more important to the resolution of our problem
than just this, that the difficulty need never have arisen at all; that
philosophers can philosophize freely and confidently with no
more self-doubt than afflicts other craftsmen. Angst does not arise in
midst of one's work or amongst one's friends, but between jobs and
in solitude. And lonely idleness is not the human condition.

The title of 'The Central Problem of Philosophy' may seem to
imply a large claim. Let me reassure or disappoint you: I do not
pretend to have solved philosophy's central problem. If it still
seems too much that I should claim to identify the centre and discuss
it, some comfort may be found in reflecting that the centre of even
the largest sphere is a single point that has no dimensions; that, if
Leibniz is to be believed, one may regard as the centre of the world
any point which it is for the time being convenient to treat as such;
and that, as may be seen from any doughnut, the centre of a thing
is not always the part of it that offers most for one to get one's
teeth into.

The Central
Problem of
Philosophy

I have never thought of myself as a philosopher. By 'philosopher' here I mean one who displays the same professional competence in his subject that professors of other subjects do in theirs: one who, when you make any philosophical remark or ask any philosophical question, can tell you at once the sixteen things it may mean, the principal articles and books in which it is discussed, the positions taken up on it by the leading authorities both living and dead, which if any of those positions are academically respectable—and, most important of all, whether what you have just said is fashionable. This competence I do not possess. When confronted with philosophical discourse I am struck all of a heap. I cannot even give a clear and straightforward answer to such elementary questions as whether the will is free or what Plato's Theory of Ideas was; and this is not, as you probably think I am trying to imply, because my mind is too subtle, but because it is too confused. As the years go by I become more glib. But it is still true, as Augustine might have said, that if somebody asks me, I know; if nobody asks me, I don't know.

This widespread and basic stupefaction used not to trouble me greatly, since I was able to represent myself to myself as one who was just filling in his time teaching a little philosophy till some more suitable occupation should suggest itself. But as time passes it gets clearer and clearer that this was an illusion, and that I am just filling in my time teaching a little philosophy. So the only excuse for my ineptitude has gone. It is up to me to diagnose and remedy my intellectual block.

The diagnosis is easy. I make no progress because I can't get started. And I can't get started because I can't make out what philosophy is about or what it is for. As for remedies, the obvious one would be to go to a dictionary, or perhaps an encyclopaedia or a textbook, where such things are explained. But this cure doesn't take. What one finds in such sources, intellectually unobjectionable though it may be, fails to carry the kind of conviction one needs in what is to be, after all, the foundation of one's life-work. Such a foundation must be something personal, and central or able to be made central to one's concern. Whatever philosophy may be, surely it cannot be just a job.

It would appear, then, that the edifice of one's philosophizing should rest on some idea, or inkling, or experience, around which thoughts cluster, and which seems or has at least for a little while seemed to provide, if not the key to the meaning of all things, at least some urgent problem that could serve as a centre for one's philosophical excursions. That should not be too hard for me to provide. Often, usually late at night, I am struck with notions which do seem to have such possibilities—to open vistas of inquiry or speculation whose end I do not see. It is my custom to scrawl these down on pieces of paper and file them. When I examine them, next morning or later, they are usually illegible and always unintelligible. I thereupon throw them away. But when I diagnosed the predicament I have outlined I thought it advisable, the next time I had such an idea, to write it down legibly and then work it up and see how far I could get with it. It happened that, very soon after the next idea came, I was asked to address a philosophical society; so I seized the opportunity to commit myself to present, on a given date, whatever the results might be in front of the enlightened but sympathetic audience who first heard what you now read. So you see that the point, not only of what I said, but of my saying it in that company and in this particular way, was in the first place a personal one. Please do not take offence at this. I would not have gone through with the project were there not also, in my judgement, a second place.

The experience which gave me my opportunity, and the reflections it aroused, were of what I gather to be a quite ordinary kind; their only importance is that they seemed important then. I had been reading a sociological article on 'Methods of Measurement of Aesthetic Folkways'[1] and brooding on its seeming faults. Its author sought an index to the fluctuations of musical taste in a statistical study of the changes in the representation of various composers in the programmes of certain symphony orchestras over several decades. He did not analyze or assess or even enumerate the factors other than taste by which composers of programmes have to be guided. He did not allude to the fact that, while the forty or so composers represented changed places often enough in the order of preference, there were many more whose works were never played at all. In the mood of exasperation induced by this reading I put a record on my record-player. Through whatever cause, the music had on me that shaking effect which great works of art sometimes do have and often do not. It at once occurred to me that this effect was the one thing above all others that the author of the article ought to have mentioned, but had not; and, further, that no theory of aesthetics, at least in its strictly theoretical part as opposed to its rhetorical trimmings, would lead one to expect an effect of quite this kind, although with the effect fresh in one's recollection one could see that this was in fact what such theories were often trying to explain.

What was this effect? I noted four things about it, none of which I could express in a form that I should accept as literally true. I recognize, looking back, that the phrases I used were current clichés, more picturesque than informative. But no language less metaphorical was available, and what I said was what the experience seemed to demand.[2] The first of the four things I noted was, that the music is *there*: *confronting* one: a 'presence,' as we say: not as something to be desired, or explained, or enjoyed, but there in its own right and sufficient to itself. The second thing was, that it has a *perfection* which one cannot imagine either exceeded or altered: there is no further to go in this direction, nothing more to be done here. The third thing was, that this perfection is something one could not have expected and *could never have deserved*. There seems to be no sound reason why deserts should be spoken of in this connection, but this was the first thing that struck me as needing to be said. It is a *gratuitous* perfection that the music has. And the fourth thing I noted was, that the work presents itself as a standard by which one is *judged*—not as something that satisfies criteria, or provides a criterion for judging other works (though in other contexts those might be the right things to say), but as a standard against which one is personally measured and falls short.

When considered in the light of the music as thus found, sociological explanations of taste seemed not so much inadequate as beside the point; and surely, I thought, for aesthetics this point of all points is the one not to be beside. The central problem of aesthetics might well be to do justice to such an experience. But how could any theory do that? One would not wish to construct a philosophical theory out of the four points just put before you, which must have seemed extravagant in what they suggest and jejune in what they say. At least, I hope they have seemed so; and I expect they have, because in the context of the experience thus considered I was able to see the point of certain theories in aesthetics which had previously seemed inept or hyperbolic. In particular, Clive Bell's famous remarks on aesthetic emotion seem, in this context, no more than reasonable.[3] And yet I cannot see that this possibility of sympathy with his feelings makes Bell's theory a good theory. Such theories as his, though not completely beside the point, certainly fail to do justice to it (however vague the criteria for done justice may be): the explanations seem incommensurate with what most of all needs explaining. In this seeming failure of aesthetic theory to measure up to the most strikingly obvious of the demands made on it I found the explanation of what had previously puzzled me: the widespread complaint that aesthetics is dreary whereas art is thrilling. This complaint is puzzling, because it is like objecting to a cook-book for not tasting good; but one can perhaps sympathize with it as a reaction to this failure. People who complain thus do not find the explanations they are offered powerful enough for the astounding fact. Their feelings may be justified, though they find an absurd way of expressing them—for they write as if they wanted all books on aesthetics to be printed in capital letters, or in red.

My next move must be to apply more generally what I have alleged of aesthetics: to see whether within the scope of other philosophical disciplines there are similar judgements or confrontations, and similar attempts and failures by philosophy to cope with them. (Here, and in all that follows, I use without system sometimes one and sometimes another of the four aspects of my experience.)

In the philosophy of science and the philosophy of history I expected to find none such. I took the former to be devoted to questions of logic and such epistemological problems as are purely technical, and the latter to be concerned with the possibility of understanding the past (which can no longer confront us) and with attempts to read pattern and meaning into trains of events which likewise cannot confront the inquirer.

To the philosophy of religion I turned with more hope. In his *Time and Western Man*, which I had just been reading, Wyndham Lewis says that what we (Wyndham Lewis) read of God we (Wyndham Lewis) experience in Mozart—an absolute perfection. So it may be that what we have found in Mozart we may read of God. Rudolf Otto, in *The Idea of the Holy*, makes the philosophy of religion centre around an experience of holiness—a *confrontation* with that which inspires awe. And it has become common to speak of God, in so far as God reveals himself to men, as a being 'Wholly Other'; possessor and bestower of a perfection beyond what we can deserve; and our judge. If those who use such terms speak honestly of what they have found, or believe others to have found, and if I have described honestly my own finding, there is here an analogy quite striking enough to justify Lewis's statement. The difference, an important one, is that in so describing a musical experience one is more conscious of metaphor than when speaking of religious experience. It is often held that God really is a judge, or something very like one; but in the musical experience, though we may find judgement, we have no judge.

The analogy between aesthetics and the philosophy of religion is far-reaching and striking, and has been much exploited though not so much discussed. Each is concerned with an aspect of human passion and action which has no known biological function, but which is none the less virtually universal (no culture without either is known ever to have existed), and to which men attach a very high value. For this reason those philosophers who are primarily concerned with what we may term the *depth* of human experience tend to make one or both of these disciplines their point of departure. Whichever is chosen, the general feel of the resulting philosophical structure is much the same. On a less pretentious level, it is possible to take what Durkheim says of the nature and function of religion and apply it to art[4]—in fact, this is often done almost unconsciously, the cases are so similar. That religions do tend to find artistic expression, and art to acquire religious significance, is generally agreed and seems evidently true; and it is a mere commonplace that people in 'our society' who forswear religion often 'make a religion' of art. In his *Prière et poésie* Henri Bremond pursues the connection between art and religion at least as far as anyone would wish to go. And H. D. Lewis, more recently, quite brazenly and habitually uses the language of theology to speak of art.[5] In general, I would say that when one is faced with a problem in aesthetics it is never a waste of time to look for an analogous problem in the philosophy of religion, and vice versa: it is on this basis that our present argument moves forward.

H. H. Farmer points out that two approaches to the philosophy of religion are possible. One may start by considering the ubiquity of religious institutions and generalizing from what is variously done, or one may start by considering the nature of what seems most vital and essential in one's own religious life and allowing the term 'religion' to be applied solely to what answers to this notion.[6] (For Farmer, this vital and essential element is that experience of the Holy of which I have spoken.) We may say of this dichotomy, that a consideration of the *ubiquity* of religious behaviour generates curiosity and raises problems which call for discussion; whereas a consideration of the *depth* of religious experience generates an amazement in which words fail. But the latter approach, as Farmer says, is the only one that does justice to our main concern. So it seems that to get anything said one is condemned to start from what doesn't greatly matter. And the same holds in aesthetics. Some theories start by considering as art the whole range of artistic expression: all the songs, carved combs, tattooings and what not of all the peoples of the world without regard to their excellence; others start by considering the greatness of great works and their effect. But here again we meet the dilemma: only the latter theories deal with what we feel is important, but only the former have anything definite to say. One has apparently to choose between a competent discussion of trivialities and a series of emotional outbursts about what matters.

This dichotomy of possible approaches, and consequently of styles, suggests that I dealt too summarily with the philosophy of history. I represented that discipline as the competent discussion, not indeed of trivialities, but of matters of less than vital concern. But there are also philosophies of history which take their start from a consideration not of all recorded happenings equally but of a single event of which they use such terms as I have used to describe my own experience. One such is Berdiaev's *The Meaning of History*. It is true that Berdiaev is not reduced to speechlessness, although he has a great deal to say about silence; but it is also true that what he does say about this crucial event looks, when unsympathetically considered, like tripe. Memorable tripe, perhaps, but tripe.

From the philosophy of religion I turned to ethics. Here the split between ubiquity and intensity, between extension and depth, was readily found. The ubiquity of morality is no less striking than that of art and religion, and again generates problems which can be and are fruitfully discussed: the meaning of ethical terms, the function of moral judgements, the authority of moral laws, the relation of morality to prudence, and the like. And when we look for an experience of that which confronts and judges, of a perfection by which we are abashed, we find not one but at least three different kinds.

First, there is saintliness of character. Saintliness is, I think, easily recognizable, and is quite different from respectability; no definition of moral virtue seems adequate or even relevant to it. It is a quality that puts one to shame, and whose importance in the moral lives of those who come across it is paramount, and which yet plays no part in most moral philosophies. It is hard to see how it could be brought in; but its absence makes ethical theory look trivial. Second, quite different from saintliness, there is heroism in action, together with the peculiar force of character called greatness. The awe-inspiringness of such a quality of deed or character is widely attested—in poetry; but again, though moral philosophers often feel called on to mention it, they seldom feel obliged to reckon with it. The classical case of its formal omission is Aristotle, who in spite of himself when defining virtue was impelled to use terms which make him seem to careless readers an advocate of half-heartedness and burgherly respectability. From a casual reading of the *Ethics* one would never guess that Aristotle wrote a poem on the heroism of Hermias in terms so extravagant as to expose himself to a charge of blasphemy; or that he could write of Plato that he was one 'whom it is not lawful for bad men even to praise'—which I take to be a typical response to saintliness.[7] As with saintliness, it is hard to see how greatness could be brought within the scope of theory. Some, such as Nicolai Hartmann, have tried; but examination of the result may make one glad that the attempt is not made more often.

Attempts to bring saintliness and greatness within the bounds of theory are found less often in ethics than in aesthetics, where discussions of 'the sublime' (common in the eighteenth century, but virtually extinct since the 1914-18 war) are perhaps best thought of as confused attempts to account for those philosophically intractable aspects of living with which this paper is concerned. What happens when such accounts are critically (rather than sympathetically) examined, with reference to what the words say rather than to what the speakers would be saying, may best be seen from E. F. Carritt's chapter on the sublime in his *Theory of Beauty*. His strictures on theories of the sublime are irrefutable: as intellectual constructions, the theories are destroyed utterly. But, just because of the incommensurability between such experience and anything that can be about them, he seems like a bull that rends a matador's cloak but thereby misses the matador.

The third type of experience I have to put alongside those of confrontation by saintliness and by heroism is one that I take on trust. It forms the foundation of a theory of ethics which, probably for that reason, has seemed to many to be the only theory of ethics worth taking seriously, and to many others to be neurotic rubbish. When I spoke of the 'judgement without a judge' in an aesthetic experience some at least among you must have thought of a law without a lawgiver: of Kant's 'Categorical Imperative.' And the experience of which I now speak is that described in the Conclusion of the *Critique of Practical Reason*: 'Two things fill the mind with ever new and increasing wonder and awe, the oftener and the more steadily we reflect on them: the starry heavens above me, and the moral law within me.' We do not have to seek these out, says Kant, we see them before us—in the terms I have been using, they confront us. I do not share this experience of the moral law, and I do not know how common it is; but the terms Kant uses of it are appropriate only to such experiences as I have described.

If I am justified in taking the experience of which I am speaking to be of central importance in philosophy, the three types of such experience in the field of morality must answer to some threefold division in the discipline of ethics. And this we do find, though the correspondence is less neat than one could wish and also a bit disconcerting. The relationship between the encounter with heroism and that with the moral law is reflected in the relationship between the good and the right, between ideals and commitments, which provides ethics with one of its major topics. The distinction between sanctity and heroism has found less systematic expression in modern times; but we find in Thomas Aquinas a distinction between habitual and infused virtues which corresponds to it, and in Augustine a distinction between the true virtues of Christians and the splendid vices of pagans which is a less polite version of the same thing.[8] This contrast between Greek-style virtue culminating in greatness and Christian-style virtue culminating in holiness is familar indeed, and one can hardly imagine a topic of profounder moral importance; but, for some reason, the precise nature of each and the relationship between them have dropped out of ethical discussion.

So far, not so bad. What is disconcerting is that the nuttiest chestnut of ethics, Kant's 'antinomy of the *summum bonum*,' the connection between virtue and happiness, has not appeared. For it to do so, there would have to be a fourth type of experience comparable to the other three: an overwhelming intimation of happiness. Such a challenging quality of bliss is hard to come by, but it is attributed to the Beatific Vision of God. The disconcertingness arises because I am tempted to preserve the symmetry of my discourse by placing this vision and the intimations thereof alongside the three other experiences as the fourth psychological foundation of ethics; and if I do that I have only to yield to the further temptation to regard such experiences as veridical, as experiences of something real, and I shall have deduced the existence of God from a theory about ethical theories. This deduction I am, pardonably I hope, reluctant to make. Hastily, therefore, I avert my gaze from ethics.

I have no recourse but to turn to metaphysics. I fasten here upon the kind of experience in which one is overwhelmingly aware of the reality, otherness, radiance and what have you of the external world, and is overtaken by what H. D. Lewis calls 'a sense of wonder that a thing should be this and not that.' It is the kind of experience that finds expression most often in recollections of childhood, as in Wordsworth's 'Ode' and the purplest passages of Traherne's *Centuries of Meditations*. The distinction between what gives rise to problems and what causes wonder, what generates talk and what is beyond talk, is here that which everyone since Aristotle (in his *Posterior Analytics*, II.7) has made between what things are and the fact of their existence—A. J. Ayer makes the same distinction in his *Philosophical Essays* by saying that indicators are not short-hand predicates. My point is made for me by Wittgenstein in the words: 'Not *how* the world is is the mystery, but *that* it is' ('Nicht *wie* die Welt ist, ist das Mystische, sondern *dass* sie ist'— *Tractatus*, 6.44). The term 'mystery' here is no mere term of abuse. Its implications are brought out in a remark in Aristotle's *On Philosophy*: that those who are initiated into mysteries are not supposed to learn anything, but to experience something. There is nothing in the world one cannot talk about and make shift somehow to describe; what words cannot do is express and convey the very actuality of things.

The notion that however accurately one describes anything one simply circles round and round the object without ever coming to grips with it in its full reality is of course Bergson's; but he is a philosopher I would rather not talk about. His style, which has charmed so many, puts me off. So I say, as newspapers say when their advertisers fail to provide copy: Space reserved for Henri Bergson. After him, the thinker who has made most use of the distinction between what things are and the fact that they exist is probably Thomas Aquinas, in so far as I can make out his very elusive theory of the relation between essence and the 'act' of existence. Aquinas' philosophy does indeed seem to be that of a man struck to the heart by the reality of things, but he was such a self-effacing writer that we cannot positively assert this of him. Our hesitation may be increased when we discover the prominence of Bergson's students among those scholars who have rescued this aspect of Thomist thought from six centuries of almost unbroken misunderstanding. However, if it is right to associate his theory of existence with experience of this kind, and if that theory has as important a place in his thought as Etienne Gilson and others maintain, we can say that such experiences were at the centre of his philosophy; and then we can trace all the misunderstandings of his theory, which in various ways assimilate existence to essence, to attempts by those who lack such experience to conceptualize what must evade all concepts.

Whatever may be the truth about Thomism, the 'awareness of the irrevocability by which a thing is what it is' (to quote H. D. Lewis for the last time) is not all that metaphysics has for us. Not only do all things have an aspect that may provide an experience of confrontation and with which words cannot cope, but some people have thought it necessary to postulate an entity which has no other aspect than this. For Aquinas this is a being, namely God, in which existence and essence cannot be distinguished, so that nothing can be said of God with literal truth except that He exists—and we don't even know quite what we mean by 'exist' here. For Plotinus it is an entity, namely the One, which is beyond reality and beyond thought, and of which nothing can be said with literal truth except that it is the cause of all other things—and even this is really not a truth about the One but a truth about all other things. Aquinas and Plotinus agree that this indescribable being can be made the object of such an experience as I am discussing. It follows that they make everything that can be discussed depend for its existence upon that which can be experienced but cannot form the object of adequate discursive thought. Philosophy is thus confined, if not to trivialities, to matters of secondary importance at most. Accordingly, we are not surprised to be told that after an experience he had while celebrating Mass in December 1273 Aquinas decided not to proceed with the third part of his *Summa Theologiae*, because in the light of his experience all that he had written seemed to him like so much straw. The wonder is that he went on so long.

At least some great metaphysicians, then, bear out by their practice and doctrine what we had inferred from the nature of the case: that the philosophical discipline which purports to take for its province everything that there is must confine its discussions to small things or the lesser aspects of great things. This restriction, though necessary, is a standing reproach to philosophy. Tertullian (*De Praescriptione Hereticorum*, VII.6) blamed it on 'That jerk Aristotle, who invented philosophy for these people: the art of setting up and knocking down, turncoat in its opinions, forced in its speculations, niggling in its arguments, a breeder of controversy, a nuisance even to itself, reconsidering everything lest it should have to consider something.' Tertullian would.

My theme is now ripe for the introduction of a little pseudo-Cartesian doubt. Not as a methodological expedient but in morbid earnest we may be asked: is all this 'otherness' and 'confrontation' not an illusion? Our experiences of 'otherness' are still *our* experiences, are they not? And if so, they are not 'other' at all: whatever we experience (or are confronted by) falls necessarily *within* our experience. This, of course, is a mere undergraduate's paradox, and one is inclined to brush it aside. Can one seriously be thought, we ask in reply, to spin out of one's own intellectual entrails that by which one seems confronted?—not to mention that by which one feels judged! But this dismissal is too hasty, for a consideration of our musical experience suggests how the apparently impossible situation could be brought about. No finished product of human thought, whether it be symphony or poem or statue or mathematical demonstration or philosophical treatise or railroad system, represents the average quality of its producer's thinking. The latter is but fitfully rational, and is neither continuously bent on the production of the artefact nor, when so bent, either always successful or uniformly coherent. A successful artefact embodies the running-together of the best moments of this process, and also of the best moments of the critical thought bent on that running-together. Hence any competent work of art or skill, *even one's own*, represents a standard by which the quality of one's unrehearsed thought-process at any time must fall short. Confronted by one's own work, one asks: 'How could *I* possibly have done that?' But one has done it. One has, in the phrase just used, spun out of one's own intellectual entrails that by which one seems confronted, and even judged. So perhaps, by analogy, it is not impossible that the Wholly Other God before whom we are abashed should be a figment of our unconscious minds; or that the world on which we blister our feet should be a product of our imagination. It always amazes me how well I dream, considering how badly I draw.

Thus, by conceding that we may be judged by nothing more than our own amplified echoes, or our own images in a non-existent mirror, we find ourselves forced into the kind of idealistic tizzy in which the boundaries between self and not-self either become blurred or, if they remain distinct, merely divide the ego from the alter ego. The German philosophies in which this fusion most notoriously takes place are also those in which man's artistic creativity has been given an important place. This is no mere coincidence. It is, as we have just seen, in artistic creation that what seems other than and greater than a man is none the less plainly his own product. In such idealisms the kind of experience from which my discussion began is important, but is not what it seems.

To avoid the idealistic tizzy, we may well wish to keep sharp the kind of distinction we usually make between individual and environment. But if we then allow full weight to our confrontations by the external world, to those moments of heightened awareness when we are so keenly awake to its reality that we are tempted to say that we are judged by it, the results are likely to be unsettling. The manipulability of the external world both in thought and in practice is a sort of guarantee that it cannot really have the kind of status it here seems to have.[9] There is a judgement whereby we are judged—but there is no judge. Such an experience lies at the heart of certain modes of atheist existentialism. When the hero in Sartre's *Nausea* looks at that root, it makes him dizzy. There is the root, set over against him, confronting him. It is excessive, it overflows the concepts one applies to roots. But of course, though Sartre doesn't say this, the realization of the root's aggressive and superabundant individuality would not have this vertiginous effect were it not that the root is, after all, only a root. It has no business to set itself up as a judge. (When *l'être pour-soi* claims the status of *l'être en-soi*, we accuse it of 'bad faith.' But what are we to say when the in-itself thus pretends to the status of the for-itself?) Curiously enough, we find another phase of this existentialist tizzy—which is quite different from the idealist tizzy, but none the less a tizzy—in *Time and Western Man*, although Lewis seems to regard himself as a follower of the good Bishop Berkeley. According to Lewis, 'The material world must . . . be imaginary: and the very effrontery of its superb solidness and the bland assurance with which it is camped before us, should actually help us to realize that' (page 478). One feels like saying 'Come off it,' but one sees what he means: that inanimate things have the fixed and brazen glare of a mask, not the continual evasiveness of a living face. Just as an immobile countenance may lead one to suspect that its owner is asleep, entranced, or dead, so here the conviction may grow that *there is nothing behind the mask*.

The failure of existentialism to make headway in the English-speaking world suggests that this notion of a world of contorted masks with Nothing behind them is to 'healthy-minded' people exotic and gratuitous nonsense. But in the context of ethics it may engage our sympathies rather more readily. I have said that in morality that by which we feel ourselves humbled is sanctity and heroism. But one is only heroic in defence of something (if only one's own name) in which one believes passionately. And sainthood comes from believing wholeheartedly in something beyond oneself. Yet the saint's belief is in 'things not seen' and his trust is not founded on trustworthiness: 'Though he slay me, yet will I trust in him.' And it is the mark of a hero that he continues his defence when he knows that it cannot succeed and is therefore pointless. Neither saint nor hero can justify his conduct by reference to an objective situation: it is rather their conduct that ratifies their beliefs. Considered abstractly, the situation may be stimulating and even joyful and liberating:

All the beauty and sublimity we have lent to real and imaginary things, I intend to reclaim as property and production of man: as his most beautiful justification. Man as poet, as thinker, as god, as love, as power—: O, the royal munificence with which he has endowed things, to *impoverish* himself and feel wretched! That was his greatest selflessness hitherto, that he admired and worshipped, and was able to conceal from himself that *he* it was, who made that which he admired.[10]

Yes, but supposing one can no longer conceal it from oneself? What could be more grotesque than to sacrifice oneself for an ideal that one knows is merely one's own invention? It is pointless to say 'I endure because I choose' if the choice itself has no justification. Yet that is how *Sartre* saw it. The men of the Resistance died for an ideal which could not be justified objectively and whose supposed justification, when they died, they could no longer remember. To live for an ideal of one's own creation may possibly be magnificent, as Nietzsche thought; to die for such an ideal is only horrible. For the atheist Sartre, the heroism and sanctity that judge us are pointless: there is a judgement without judge and without justice. There is nothing behind the mask.

We have now reached the watershed of our discussion. Let us proceed downhill. . . .

There is a sense in which any experience to which our concepts are adequate, and any experience whatever in so far as our concepts are adequate to it, may be said to be 'under our control' or mastered by us. In so far as we can understand, describe or explain an experience adequately, we have obviously in some manner reduced it to our measure.[11] Experiences of which we feel we are judged by them are necessarily those to which we feel our words and thoughts inadequate. But what cannot be adequately thought about is unintelligible, ungraspable, and therefore, so far as we are concerned, indefinite. For such presocratic thinkers as Anaximander and (more explicitly) Parmenides, only what is definite can exist: whatever is indefinite is nonexistent, we are wrong to think that there can be any such thing in reality. For this way of thinking, whatever 'judges' our thought by transcending or evading our concepts must be, simply, nothing; or rather, Nothingness—*das Nichts*. Among the existentialists, Martin Heidegger has explicitly appealed to the example of these primitive thinkers. For him, the ungiven 'given,' the ultimate what-there-is that transcends our knowledge, is simply *das Nichts*; and *das Nichts*, as we all know, *nichtet*. Behind the mask of things is not merely a void, but an aching void. The position of man in such a world is not only absurd, but painfully absurd. We can be judged only by what transcends us; and what transcends us must be unsayable; and what is unsayable is nothing.

Well—who cares? But we do care that what is unsayable is *for philosophy* nothing. And is this not true? Must we not agree with whoever it was who said of the mystic Jakob Boehme that 'if Jacob had experienced the inexpressible, Jacob should not have tried to express it'? Aristotle posed this problem (*De Partibus Animalium*, 1.5), without apparently realizing its implications as Plato had done and Plotinus was to do:

The scanty perceptions to which we can attain of celestial things give us, from their excellence, more delight than all our knowledge of the world in which we live. . . . On the other hand, in certitude and completeness our knowledge of terrestrial things has the advantage.

'The higher, the fewer.' But if you go high enough don't you perhaps come to something about which there is nothing that can be known, and which therefore escapes the philosopher? The conclusion has, as we have seen, been drawn. But the scope of my present argument is far wider. In our awareness of anything whatever, it has seemed, there is something which escapes description—which we do not even feel tempted to try to describe; and in the experiences which seem most significant to those people who find significance in some of their experiences, this unsayable aspect is uppermost. What's a poor fellow to do?

Wittgenstein's answer was short and looked simple: *Wovon man nicht sprechen kann, darüber muss man schweigen*—'whereof one cannot speak, thereof one must be silent' (*Tractatus*, 7). The advice is irreproachable, but it has something of the air of a prudent evasion. Its irreproachableness and evasiveness together may serve to explain what otherwise seems inexplicable: the mutual contempt of the logical analysts, who mostly adhere to this policy, and the metaphysicians or friends of metaphysics, who don't—or rather (since metaphysics is more praised than practised), don't think they ought to. What is puzzling about this contempt is the grotesqueness of the misunderstandings which always go with it. This cannot be a mere difference of opinion, but must involve some fundamental difference of attitude or approach strong enough to produce temporary blindness. And in fact the irritations which give rise to misunderstanding can here be traced to different attitudes to what can be said. The analysts must seem to the metaphysicians to be living in a fool's paradise of triviality and evasion, because they habitually speak as if no such problem as ours existed. *Ubi solitudinem faciunt, pacem appellant*: they make a desert and call it peace. They achieve equanimity by destroying the sense of wonder in which (said Plato) philosophy begins. Since they regard it as the whole of a serious thinker's job to state and elucidate plain facts, they are apt to misrepresent all expressions of wonder or perplexity as requests for information, and then pretend to be at a loss to tell what sort of information is being requested. Misrepresentation and pretence are alike deliberate, an oblique way of suggesting that the supply and demand of information is the only decent commerce; but such philosophers do affect to believe that all metaphysical constructions are attempts to comply with such requests. It isn't that they don't have or won't admit having the experiences which give us our problem, but they think that philosophy should take no account of them. To their opponents, this attitude looks less like self-abnegation than complacent pettiness. The irritation is understandable. And yet, how right they are not to try to say the unsayable! What could be more sensible and even noble than this renunciation of claptrap? The analysts for their part are infuriated to see their metaphysically-inclined colleagues time and time again crashing the sense-barrier without even noticing that it is there, spattering their pages with such terms as 'infinite,' 'ultimate,' 'transcendent,' and the like, without any sense of intellectual responsibility, beating their mental chests for sheer delight in the hollow sound that ensues. They bring disrepute on philosophy by making claims for it which they do not attempt to fulfil, which no one could possibly fulfil, which it is patently silly even to think of fulfilling. To behave thus they must be quite indifferent to the truth of what they are saying, an unconcern which of all vices is the most horrifying to the serious thinker. This accusation too is justified. And yet, is it not an honest thinker's part, even at the risk of making a fool of himself, to struggle against the limitations of his method and storm the ineffable heights and unplumbable depths? Should he not cope as best he can with all that concerns him, rather than make his methodological purism an excuse for cheerfully omitting the greater part of his own experience?

It seems that both parties are in error, though we can sympathize with both. But then, what recourse have we? We seem to be committed to exploring and charting, without crossing, the limits of the sayable. 'Philosophy,' said Wittgenstein, 'should delimit the unthinkable from within, through the thinkable—it will indicate the unsayable by clearly setting forth the sayable' (*Tractatus*, 4.114-4.115). This was Kant's problem too, and Kant's solution to it. The attitude recommended is that of the man pictured by Lucretius as standing at the outermost edge of a finite universe, poised ready to hurl outward an experimental spear: a position unlikely to yield practical results, but full of theoretical interest. But perhaps the Kantian balance is too delicate to be maintained. One either slides back or topples over. And in any case, can it be philosophy's task merely to strike an attitude? It would not, indeed, be merely ridiculous to say so: that philosophy's prime task is to be not, as Locke and Carnap thought, science's pander, but science's bad conscience, and continually to remind reason that there are an infinity of things which surpass it; or, that essence is not existence. Or, if you will, to be like the bad man in a Western who keeps shooting round the feet of respectable citizens to make them dance.

This conclusion, however, is not inevitable. The dictum of Wittgenstein on which it rests is not, as it seems to be, a mere application of the law *tertium non datur*, but the assertion of an opinion which is plainly false. The *sprechen* whose possibility the argument precludes is the bare assertion of plain facts without purpose or context; and it is not true that one must either speak thus or be silent—indeed, one seldom speaks thus. One may, for example, drop hints. Even in the exact sciences, N. R. Campbell assures us,[12] 'A theory is valuable, and is a theory in any sense important for science, only if it evokes ideas which are not contained in the laws which it explains.' If even physical theories, then, function less by stating facts than by drawing one's attention to possibilities, we can scarcely forbid the philosopher to try to do something about the unsayable. Indeed, I think this may be regarded without absurdity as the central problem, or constellation of problems, of philosophy: not *how to say* the unsayable, but *what to do* about it.

More precisely, and therefore more confusingly, the problem is this. There fall within the purview of certain philosophical disciplines (aesthetics, philosophy of religion, ethics, metaphysics) experiences or objects of experience of which the following seems true: a philosophy which ignores them or prescinds from them is condemned to aridity or triviality, and may quite fairly be accused of evading the most important issues in its field; but a philosophy which treats of them either falls into an uninstructive and merely tiresome rhetoric, or makes statements which, though they may be true, so fail to be adequate to their subject-matter that unless one reads them with a vivid sense of the kind of experience to which they refer one cannot make sense of them at all, and which on the other hand cannot be properly integrated with the more pedestrian and systematic parts of one's discourse. And this quandary arises, not through anyone's negligence, but through the very nature of the experiences in question. How is the philosopher to cope with it?

In saying that this is the central problem of philosophy, I am claiming that different approaches to it, different attitudes towards it and different degrees of awareness of it determine, or are at least an index of, differences of approach and attitude and different degrees of sophistication in philosophy in general. Such a proposition can scarcely be proved; I leave it to your leisured consideration. What I have briefly said of various philosophers will indicate the kind of evidence I should regard as appropriate.

Now, look here, you will doubtless be saying, it is time we stopped horsing around: if this is your central problem, what are you going to do about it? But at this point my shoulders droop. I have nothing to say. At best, I hover around the problem like a candle-flame round a moth. So far as I am concerned, at the centre of philosophy, as at the centre of the field of vision, is a blind spot.

Perhaps the most appropriate action would be to write poems. Ever since Coleridge, people have been saying that poetry's job is to deal with those aspects of the world that escape the more direct methods of prose. But that is no help to us. Poet and philosopher both speak responsibly, but their responsibilities are not the same. Philosophy cannot solve its problems by ceasing to be philosophy. And poetry does not 'deal with' its subject matter in such a way that the result can be integrated with what the philosopher has done. So it looks as if philosophy can do nothing here but, as I suggested, keep the sore places of knowledge sore. Yet in saying this I seem to myself rather like the rustic who visited a great city and was gazing about him when a boy inserted in his gaping mouth a handy piece of horse-dung. He said to the boy: 'I shan't chew it, and I shan't swaller it. I shall just stand here and wait for a policeman.' The question one would have asked that rustic, and the question I ask myself, is: Why don't you spit it out?

Let us now conclude by returning to the individual predicament in the context of which I placed this discussion. The experience, and the ideas connected therewith, which were to serve as a foundation for my philosophical constructions, have been chased through almost the whole gamut of philosophical concerns; and I brought into the discussion a collection of names which only ignorance and idleness kept from being much longer. But how has this helped me? Not only am I left just as confused as ever by the problem whose ramifications I have explored, but the confusion it has left me in is of the same kind as that in which I started. Given this problem, I still see no way of getting started on its solution. The supposed cure for philosophical paralysis has proved no more successful than looking 'philosophy' up in a dictionary. Perhaps what was in error was the diagnosis itself. Perhaps what I had taken for an inability to philosophize was simply a particular style of philosophizing—the style imposed on me by habits of thinking which I am not able to alter. 'From nothing *in the field of sight*,' writes Wittgenstein, 'can it be inferred that it is seen from an eye' (*Tractatus*, 5.633). And that is how I came to overlook this obvious conclusion. So perhaps I had better thrust myself back in the purgatorial fire, as T. S. Eliot recommends, and abandon the illusion that there is any technique with whose aid a philosopher of one kind can change himself into a philosopher of a different kind.

Perhaps that was a bit sudden. What has just happened is this: the realization that after a lot of fairly constructive philosophizing one was still where one began, bouncing up and down to test the springs, has suggested that to be always beginning is one way of philosophizing. William of Ockham is not the only philosopher to have earned the title of Venerabilis Inceptor, the Old Beginner. It remains to generalize this thought, to consider whether philosophy may not be, by its own nature, the discipline in which one is always beginning. That would certainly explain why, as Tertullian complained, philosophy so seldom reaches agreed conclusions.

What is the starting point from which this beginning is perpetually renewed? If thought cannot be of vital significance unless it has a personal context, but cannot be philosophically effective unless the context is that of an artificially cultivated persona, perhaps all that philosophy does is to explore the potentialities of the role of philosopher. If that is so, the restriction on the sayable that philosophy 'examines from within' will not be one imposed by the limitations of discourse as such but one self-imposed by the philosophical attitude.

The impetus of the ritual of riddling, the momentum of philosophical habit, puts philosophy in danger of reducing itself to a study of its own processes. That would imprison the discipline in a vicious regress, than which nothing could be less effectively mobile: it is small comfort that Aristotle attributed a similar self-absorption to the Unmoved Mover. But in fact philosophy, for all its lack of progress, keeps visibly on the move. How does it manage to do so?

The answer could be that the philosopher, in asking 'What is philosophy?' is asking not only what he has done and is doing but what he is to do next. And it is this possibility that the next essay explores. It does so by picking up a conceit thrown out earlier, that we may feel that we are submitted to judgement by 'our own image in a non-existent mirror.'

What comes now of our quest for salvation? It seems that the logic of redemption as theologians know it extends even to such secular contexts as our own: that the philosopher is justified through faith rather than by his works is one implication of 'The Central Problem of Philosophy.' But we are also told that faith without works is dead, and that no doubt will turn out to be a philosophical truth as well. Emil Fackenheim reminds us that to many philosophers human life is self-making: each man in his own lifetime makes his own character, nations in their history forge their own nationality, and human history as a whole is the record of the self-making of man.[1] So, too, each author by his own authority and each philosopher by his philosophizing makes himself into just the author or philosopher that he is. The persona that he expresses is one that it may seem to him that he discovers and that in fact he makes. And this after all is very comforting, for it shows that the philosophical grail-journey, if made in earnest, is not merely self-justifying but is actually bound to succeed. And, if it is undertaken in irony or despair, this its mood will itself doubtless turn out to have been its destination. Thus faith is what works.

Such success as we have just described, the success of a quest that ends in discovering its own product, would be ambiguous indeed. To proclaim it a true success would itself be an act of faith: it would make a system of arbitrariness. That is why we must go on to generalize the results that we have now obtained. We must ask whether the self-making of a philosopher does not have an inevitable dialectic of its own, so that philosophers as philosophers, no less than men as men, have a common 'nature' that is no less ineluctable than the unique individuality of each of them. This shared nature would be determined by their shared commitment in a shared situation.

Speculation and Reflection

Or: It's All Done By Mirrors

For every philosopher, in every age, the first question must be: just what is philosophy? It is agreed that its perennial chore is to explore the limits of human thinking and the proper deployment of reason within those limits; but it follows that, if he could determine with accuracy and certainty the limitations and proper methods of his own activity, the philosopher would already have completed a major part of his task. It is therefore not surprising that this initial question is never answered to everyone's satisfaction. It seems that philosophy is in large measure its own subject. What kind of business, then, does it turn out to be?

Insofar as philosophy goes beyond its necessary but seemingly non-committal functions of analyzing and criticizing, its procedures may without absurdity be characterized as *speculation* and *reflection*. But reflecting is, of course, what mirrors do; so that, if we were so ignorant as to derive the term 'speculation' from the Latin *speculum*, which means a mirror, we might go on to say that philosophy in its freer flights depends on the use of mirrors.

What you are most likely to see if you look into a mirror is your own face. No harm in that: self-knowledge is always valuable, and people who can see their faces are able to keep them cleaner and tidier than they otherwise might. But mirrors do have other uses too. It is by using mirrors that commanders of submarines escape the ignorance that is the usual consequence of submersion; it is with mirrors, suitably arranged, that dumpy persons at the backs of crowds are able to glimpse royalty riding by; searchlight crews use mirrors to bring their illumination into focus and make their observations more penetrating, and astronomers use them to obtain a record of remote and nebulous objects. So we may well ask: is philosophical thought reflexive as well as reflective? Does philosophy see in its mirror the stars, or merely its own face?

There are three questions that might be put in this form, two of which I leave aside. One thing I do not want to ask is whether philosophers' theories reflect the presuppositions of their own social and economic class. By a judicious selection and arrangement of explanatory gimmicks, anything any philosopher says can be shown to be characteristic of any class, whether he belongs to it or not, and it is beyond my powers to select a gimmick that will give only true answers. Nor do I want to ask whether men, in trying to think about the world, are not really thinking only about themselves—whether the human mind in its investigations discovers the nature of a reality other than itself or simply its own constitution and the laws that govern its own workings. It matters little which way that question is answered: it comes to the same thing in the end. Parmenides long ago said 'To be, and to be thought about, are one and the same.' Or did he perhaps say 'Only what can think can exist?' Or even 'Thinking and being are the same?' A certain crankiness in his venerable syntax, perhaps even in his venerable character, prevents us from ever being quite sure.[1] But in any case, if we begin with the world, we can know it only in the aspect which it presents for our knowledge; and if we start with our knowledge, whatever we have knowledge of is properly called 'the world'. So instead of posing this unreal alternative between world-knowledge and man-knowledge I would rather assert that if philosophy's first problem is the nature of philosophy, its last problem is the nature of man and his world. And this turns out to be one problem, not two. On the one hand, to ask about the nature of the world is to ask about the environment in which men live, and the nature of an environment as such depends on the nature of those whose environment it is. On the other hand, what we take the nature of man to be will be determined by what we think is the nature of the world in which men live.

This compound problem, of the nature of man and of his world, is not a factual one but deliberative: one to be settled, that is, not by finding things out but by making up one's mind. There are, of course, hard facts that determine what answers to the question are admissible, but it is not these facts that are in question. There are many ways in which, many aspects under which, we men can think about ourselves, and about the world considered as our environment, without committing detectable errors of fact. So the question 'What is man?' becomes 'What shall we make of man?'; and this in both senses of that expression: 'What shall we take ourselves to be?' and 'What shall we become?' And since the answer to the question 'What kind of a world is it in which we find ourselves?' both governs and depends upon the answer to the question about man, it is itself in part likewise deliberative, and in part modifies the extent to which the other is so. Almost all the detailed questions that philosophers discuss are tributary to these first and last questions, and so are deliberative like them, though if the detail is fine enough their deliberative side need never come to the fore.

Those, then, are the questions I do not want to raise. What question do I want to raise? It is one whose necessity and purport I can best make plain by elaborating and qualifying what I have just said about the deliberative nature of philosophical questions. For philosophers do not usually intend their thinking to be deliberative. They have traditionally aspired to objective truth, and claimed that their inquiries were designed to make man and his world intelligible as they are, and not as we should like them to be. I have suggested that these aspirations are misdirected. But, if they are, how do they come to be formed? Well, first, how are they directed? To what kind of understanding do they aspire? For there are two different kinds, if Aristotle is to be believed, which seldom coincide. A thing may be intelligible in itself, or intelligible to us. What is intelligible to us is what is familiar, what falls within our common experience and approximates to everyday notions. We call it intelligible only because we are so used to it that it fails to puzzle us. What is intelligible in itself, on the other hand, is whatever can be unambiguously, adequately and exactly grasped and expressed; and this may be something very unfamiliar and strange. While our everyday notions resist precise formulation, what is perfectly clear in itself is likely to be hard for an untaught mind to understand. The philosopher's project of making man and his world intelligible is presumably directed to this latter, difficult kind of clarity; and, if so, it must be expected to end in something remote from common notions. Indeed, if it did not there would be no call for philosophy at all. But then, if this remote and unfamiliar truth is the truth about man as he really is, surely we ought to live by it. Even if philosophers do not think of their task as deliberative, we cannot suppose that the real truth about ourselves is irrelevant to what decisions we ought to make. Yet, no matter what the philosophers may say, we all, including the philosophers, go on living in accordance with common, familiar ideas about human life. So Kierkegaard complains in *The Sickness Unto Death* that a systematic philosopher is like a man who builds a castle and then lives next door to it in a shack.[2]

On reflection, Kierkegaard's complaint seems foolish. After all, the builders of the Saint Lawrence Seaway, of Amiens and Chartres, did not go to live in their cathedrals and canals, and would have been thought decidedly odd if they had. Even castles are designed more for safety in sieges than for domestic comfort. So, if one cannot, with the best will in the world, however well trained one's mind and however well one knows them, think for practical purposes in terms of the system of a Hegel or a Parmenides, where is the harm? Why should the decisions affected by such visions not be confined to theoretical ones? If that is conceded, philosophical questions about man and his world will be involuntarily deliberative not in the sense that any answer to them must embody guidance for behaviour, but only in the sense that the answer to be given must be a matter for choice. The choice may be taken on grounds relevant to theory only, not at all to practice.

What, then, is the substance of Kierkegaard's objection to such purely theoretical constructions? To answer that, we must look at our other question: how philosophers' inquiries, if they are really deliberative, could be mistaken for factual ones. Surely philosophers are not all foolish, and it is odd that a man should take himself to be making discoveries when what he is really making is decisions. The answer is that, as I have already remarked, a philosopher, in propounding such questions in however veiled a form, is not free and does not conceive himself to be free to say anything he pleases about them. There are facts about man and his world to which whatever he may say is expected to conform: what he says should be neither false nor inappropriate. His questions are deliberative in the sense that these controlling facts are innumerable and various, and his answers depend on what facts he gives most weight to; but his claim will always be that no other weighting of the facts will admit an answer so truthful and appropriate as his. He knows that others prefer their own weighting to his, but cannot find it in his heart to believe that this is more than a passing fancy: reason will soon prevail, and the merits of his own version will make their invincible way. But what is it that his account is so appropriate to? Surely, to the nature of human life: what else? And this is something with which we are all familiar, with which in a sense we are all equally familiar. For the nature of human life is nothing more than the way people live, which is something we all do all the time. It was in an uncharacteristically subtle moment that Democritus, confronted with simplifying definitions of man as a 'tame rational animal' or 'flat-clawed featherless biped' or what not, replied that 'Man is—what we all know.'[3] For our experience of humanity is nothing less than the whole of our experience, and cannot be summarized or reduced to any phrase or formula. And because human life is something we know, by living it, better and more fully than it could conceivably be represented by any discourse, however refined or extended,[4] the distinction between what is intelligible in itself and what is intelligible to us can here have no application. All extravagant theoretical accounts of man are thus shown to be inadequate and inappropriate, and the philosopher is reduced to reminding us of, and making clear to us, what we already confusedly know. What he says then should after all be relevant to our task of being human; and what Kierkegaard is complaining of is that what philosophers have conceived themselves compelled by logic and fact to say does not bear on that task, that the facts to which they are faithful are apparently chosen on other grounds. But what other grounds could be appropriate? I suggested that such an account might be justified by its relevance to 'theoretical decisions.' But really that is no answer at all; for the only theoretical decisions that could be relevant are those relating to a theory about man and his world. And surely, if an account of man and his world is remote from common experience, it cannot be man and his world that it is an account of.—It is all very perplexing.

Karl Jaspers, expatiating in *Reason and Existenz* upon Kierkegaard's aphorism about the castle and the shack, says that 'The thought of a man must be the house in which he lives or it will become perverted.'[5] But what then becomes of Jaspers' own thought? For it seems that he, like most existentialists, thinks that the true nature of humanity is obscured in everyday life and clearly revealed only in situations of intellectual or emotional crisis, when social complacency is shaken. And this seems a reasonable enough view. In our less guarded moments at least, surely we all do think of ourselves and our surroundings in terms that are purely conventional, reflecting no reality, not even that of the social order to which we belong, but only prejudices and cant phrases that save us the trouble of looking and pondering. We wallow habitually in a slough of pretence and illusion, of silly cares and vain ambitions. We can lift ourselves out of this morass only briefly, and only far enough to see what a mess we are in; then our nerve fails, and we sink back. This human weakness has consequences for my argument that are most unfortunate. For it seems that, if a philosopher departs from common notions, what he says is inappropriate to the human condition; if he follows common notions, he succeeds only in conforming to a vulgar mythology that even its victims despise.

There is one obvious way for the philosopher to get himself out of the predicament in which our argument has located him: that he should acknowledge to the full the deliberative nature of the questions he asks, and go to live in the castle he has built. If the beliefs of the multitude are mistaken, and yet appropriate to the life they live, it seems reasonable to conclude that they must be living wrongly. So Plato concluded; so Sartre concludes. But if that is what philosophers should do, it is obviously absurd of us to offer courses in philosophy to university undergraduates, and especially to those not living in residence. We expect, or pretend to expect, these young people to think philosophically while living unphilosophically: to pretend, while they are, as we absurdly say, 'doing' philosophy, that they and their world are quite other than what in all their other thought and activity they must take them to be. How can they fulfil so ridiculous a demand? Surely they must either refuse (very sensibly) to think philosophically at all, or else embrace philosophy at the cost of social and personal disorientation. If what I have said of philosophy is true, it must either take up the whole of a person's life or be rigidly excluded. Whatever philosophy can be, it cannot be a 'subject' among other 'subjects.'

The extent of the demands made by philosophy is better understood in the fabled East. To become a philosopher in India, the story goes, one must renounce all worldly occupations, adopt clothing distinctive of one's sect, and by the prescribed exercises of yoga endeavour to orient oneself appropriately to the truth imparted by one's *guru*. Or one enters a monastery and submits to a discipline designed to pry one loose from unphilosophical distractions and illusions. Nor is this a peculiarity of the Indians: the world over, this is how the search for final truth has usually been conducted. Diogenes Laertius solemnly relates, as historic events, the innovations in the dress and hair-style that characterized the Hellenistic sects, and Dio Chrysostom wrote:

There is one style of dress for the philosopher, and another for laymen; and the same is true of their repose, their exercise, their bathing, and their whole way of life. It is the man who follows the philosophers' usage in these who must be thought of as devoting his attention to philosophy; the man who is no different in these respects, and who is not altogether unlike the multitude, must be deemed one of the latter.[6]

Even in the occidental present, it seems, the mysteries of what passes for Zen Buddhism cannot be penetrated by those who have not donned the uniform of the Beat or Hip and taken their vow of poverty, disobedience and unchastity.

Something has gone very wrong with the argument here. I have already acknowledged, and a quick eavesdrop at any philosophical convention will confirm, that philosophers, however outrageous in their speculations, are quite ordinary in their lives and interests. The demand made of those poor philosophy students, that they should think one way and live another, may be absurd; but it cannot be impossible of fulfilment, since these professional philosophers have all fulfilled it. It may be said, of course, that they ought not to have done so; that, if the image of man they develop is better or truer than that of ordinary social man, they should make themselves over in that image; and if it is no better and no truer it is a waste of time to develop it. But surely it is a little rash to suggest that so many respectable gentlemen are all unworthy of their high calling. If our argument has made us think that, it must have misled us either about the nature of that calling or about what it means to be worthy of it.

Perhaps the reason why philosophers, when not philosophizing, are ordinary people, is that there is really no other kind of person to be. While the philosopher lives among laymen, none of the physical and social pressures that impinge on them fail to impinge on him with equal force. If he lives in a cave or a monastery, he has only exchanged one non-philosophical environment for another, and will soon relapse into the routine of an ordinary monk or an ordinary troglodyte. The trappings with which exotic sects have proclaimed their emancipation from illusion are only the appurtenances of a more subtle self-deception. Even the Indian in his saffron robe must submit to the illusion of the world's multiplicity that he denounces, or he could not tell saffron from any other colour, nor find the many words in which his denunciation is expressed. Yet it seems that to this life that social man, including the social philosopher, is bound to live, philosophical images of man and philosophical constructions generally are ill suited. To what, then, are they appropriate? I suggest that they are appropriate to the activity of philosophizing itself, and to man as a being capable of philosophizing. And this, at long last, is the sense in which I want to ask whether philosophy does more than hold up the mirror to itself.

Sartre declares in *Existentialism is a Humanism* that in what we make of our lives each one of us shows what he takes the nature of man to be, and that humanity has no nature beyond what it is thus taken to be by individuals in the framing of their own life-projects.[7] If that is right, it is perfectly appropriate that a philosopher should formulate an image of man and his world that answers to his own life-project of philosophizing. This is equally true whether his philosophizing really is his way of being, as in our imagined orient, or whether his being a philosopher is just one role that he adopts among others, as in our western world. For if 'Man is what we all know' by being men, and is the whole of what we know, it is only man-as-philosopher that the philosopher can know; and all the time he is philosophizing, his experience is not of man in general, but of philosophizing man.

If the content of philosophy reflects the activity of philosophizing, it becomes plain how, in a society in which the philosopher's is just one role among others that a man for the time being adopts, it can after all be imparted to the young burgher without the exorbitant demands and embarrassing consequences I spoke of. In thinking philosophically, however reluctantly, intermittently and unsuccessfully, students are familiarizing themselves with the pattern of behaviour to which the theses that they are struggling to comprehend are related. And that explains why, as is well known, most students find philosophy impenetrably baffling for the first year or two; and then, if they persevere, quite suddenly come to find it not baffling at all. And as soon as they stop philosophizing they naturally shed the view that mirrored that activity, and thus suffer no social incapacitation at all. Our modern novelists and social scientists have taught us one thing that the ancients never knew: how easily and completely a man can slip from one social role to another.

If philosophical views reflect the philosophical activity, we can understand how it is that a philosopher like Parmenides can be satisfied with a world-view that is only theoretically and not practically viable: at all the times when he is thinking philosophically, theoretical decisions are the only ones he is taking. But at the same time we find ourselves obliged to say that insofar as philosophical images of man and his world reflect only a role of their propounders they are not super-social but sub-social, they reflect not something beyond society but a mere fragment of social reality; they depart from common notions not by becoming more exalted or truer but by leaving almost everything out. The statement that philosophy is its own first subject begins to sound less innocent than it did.

It is not hard to say what a supposed view of man that was really a view of the philosophical activity would be like. First, it would make thinking the chief of human activities: man would be a rational animal. Second, thought would be a truer guide to reality than perception, since a man can philosophize most easily when he is not looking at anything and no one is talking to him. Third, since one cannot philosophize effectively while eating or making love, pleasures of the body would be judged inferior to pleasures of the mind. Fourth, since philosophy is only one kind of activity, and a very cheap kind at that, a simple and frugal life would be extolled and a various and luxurious one condemned. And fifth, since nothing much that goes on around one need disturb one's philosophizing, change, time and movement would be dismissed as unimportant if not illusory. And is this not exactly what has been consistently palmed off on us down the centuries as a view of life higher and truer than the ordinary, to which by great gifts of intellect and character we might manage to penetrate? But now we see that it is nothing more than the way life will come to seem if one spends most of one's time shut up in one's study, speculating and reflecting. The philosopher has not built a palace beside his shack: he has only moved into an unheated and unfurnished closet inside the shack he already has.

In order to discover that one could doubt everything but the fact of one's own consciousness, Descartes first cut himself off from all social contacts (by joining the army), and then shut himself up all day in a stuffy *poêle*.[8] The intention was to avoid interruptions to his train of thought; but the effect was to provide a pure specimen of what he was seeking. Cartesianism is the philosophy of solitary confinement, where man as 'thinking substance' is cut off from the world of 'extended substance'. In his essay on 'Cartesianism', Edward Caird gave this game away:

In Malebranche, Cartesianism found an interpreter whose meditative spirit was fostered by the cloister . . . In Spinoza it found one who was in spirit and position more completely isolated than any monk, who was removed from the influence of the religious as well as the secular world of his time, and he in his solitude seemed scarcely ever to hear any voice but the voice of philosophy. It is because Cartesianism found such a pure organ of expression that its development is, in some sense, complete and typical. Its principles have been carried to their ultimate result. . . .[9]

Quite so. But the end of this road is merely the back of the cupboard.

That philosophical constructions are better suited to the study than to the living-room is no news. 'I dine,' wrote David Hume, 'I play a game of backgammon, I converse, and am merry with my friends; and when after three or four hours' amusement, I would return to these speculations, they appear so cold, and strain'd, and ridiculous, that I cannot find in my heart to enter into them any farther.'[10] But Hume still thought that what suited the study must be somehow truer and better than what was necessary at the gaming table. It may be that Dr. Samuel Johnson called this bluff in his famous attempt to refute Berkeley's 'ingenious sophistry to prove the non-existence of matter . . . I observed,' says Boswell, 'that though we are satisfied his doctrine is not true, it is impossible to refute it. I never shall forget the alacrity with which Johnson answered, striking his foot with mighty force against a large stone, until he rebounded from it—"I refute it thus." '[11] This is generally taken to be a piece of stupidity on the Doctor's part, as if he thought that sensations of touch were somehow less truly sensations than those of sight. And so it may have been. But then again it may not. For Johnson did not fondle the rock with his toes. He kicked it, so hard that he bounced: he took action in a resisting world. And, whatever the logic of the matter, it is certainly true that Berkeley would not have written as he did if he had started by thinking of men as agents in the world rather than as spectators of it. Berkeleian man is not, it is true, so ludicrously passive as Humeian man. 'The mind,' wrote Hume 'is a kind of theatre, where several perceptions successively make their appearance; pass, re-pass, glide away, and mingle in an infinite variety of postures and sensations.'[12] Who outside the study could think thus? We should be unable to take such stuff seriously at all, were it not that we are usually sitting still when we read it.

At first sight experience seems to bury us under a flood of external objects, pressing upon us with a sharp importunate reality, calling us out of ourselves in a thousand forms of action. But when reflexion begins to act upon these objects they are dissipated under its influence; the cohesive force seems suspended like some trick of magic; each object is loosed into a group of impressions—colour, odour, texture—in the mind of the observer. And if we continue to dwell in thought on this world, not of objects in the solidity with which language invests them, but of impressions, unstable, flickering, inconsistent, which burn and are extinguished with our consciousness of them, it contracts still further: the whole scope of observation is dwarfed into the narrow chamber of the individual mind.

Thus Walter Pater.[13] So daunting, we observe, is the weight of philosophical tradition, that even in the act of revealing the trickery by which the scope of observation is dwarfed he is ready to concede that the narrow chamber is the only proper place to be. No wonder the philosophers who have taken the external world of common life most seriously were the peripatetics—the philosophers who retained the use of their legs. Certainly, Humeian man never uses them, never stirs from the narrow chamber. Berkeleian man is not quite such a recluse: he does get out into Trinity College garden, and even walks far enough to see whether a distant tower is round or square.[14] But he does not fell trees: he leaves unmarked the landscape through which he drifts.

Philosophers, just because they reflect on man's nature, find that it is man's nature to be reflective. One cannot think about humanity without thinking, and it seems that the activity of thought has its own momentum and generates its own view of man. But this puts the philosopher in a situation that appears to be hopeless: if he is false to his own experience he obviously has nothing else that he can be true to, but in being true to his own experience he is being false to that of everyone else. Philosophers in the past have said, when they realized this, that all men other than philosophers are befooled by an illusion, or wandering in a dream. But no just man will thus pretend that his necessity is his virtue, and no sensible man would expect to get away with the pretence if he did. As Plato himself admitted, a philosopher's exaltation of the mind is nothing but self-praise.[15]

Things may not be so bad as I have made them look. Perhaps reflection can be so controlled that it does not distort. Philosophers are free agents, and once they recognize that the momentum of their thinking carries them in the direction I have described they set about devising remedies. One such expedient is that tried by the French existentialists, Gabriel Marcel and Jean-Paul Sartre, who supplement their theoretical works with novels, plays and journals in which the aspects of human life that they wish to emphasize are embodied and displayed. Indeed, some of the emphasis they require is carried by this very choice of narrative rather than expository form. For it is only by a narrative presentation that the temporality of human existence can be effectively conveyed, with its implication that to any man what he is now is less real than what, through his own choice, he is becoming. By using a narrative form, too, one calls in the concrete imagination to counterbalance the abstractive intellect. In a work of fiction excessive abstraction and schematization are glaringly evident; but such falsification may escape notice in a philosophical treatise, since it is only by abstraction that theoretical work can proceed at all. In a narrative presentation there is no argument, which could sail away in any direction from its enclosed premises, but an image, which invites us to compare it at each point with our intimate knowledge of the life it images. And finally the flow of life that the narrative presents or suggests has the quality of continuity that our living has, instead of the discontinuity of isolated and selected facts and generalizations. Our experience is not made up out of facts, events, and relations, but is a continuum in which indefinitely many facts, events, and relationships can be located; it is this denseness of texture, this superabundance, that evades more than anything else the scope of any possible theory.

Yet, as a philosophical device, the resort to depiction fails. The better the narratives the more they become literature as opposed to philosophy, for literature is neither a form of philosophy nor a substiute for it, but something else entirely. If its methods are different, that is because the criteria of its success are different, too. By appealing to the imagination the narrator abandons argument, renounces proof in favour of persuasion. A novel cannot be refuted. But it is by argument and refutation that philosophy lives. And whatever is irrefutable is *ipso facto* unprovable too. If the function of the existentialist's didactic narrative is simply to reproduce life as it is lived, he need not have gone to so much trouble. We have enough of that in our own experience. But if it is designed to support a thesis, should not the thesis be brought into the open? For the imagination is not less easily carried away by a plausible image than the mind by a tricky argument. To one who knows their doctrines, the fictions of the existentialists tend to become unconvincing except in those passages in which no relevance to the philosophical issues can be discovered; elsewhere, one is only too conscious that the tale is being manipulated, an awareness that kills conviction. Existentialism, in fact, never did succeed in formulating a method adequate to its insights, and that is no doubt why it has become extinct.[16]

Solutions to a philosophical predicament can only be found within philosophy. And the most obvious way would seem to be to install a corrective device to prevent speculative builders from raising their structures too high on too narrow a base, and from supporting what ought to be founded on the common ground of human experience on that slippery basis, the philosophical enterprise alone. Among such precautionary techniques the one nowadays most widely used is that known as 'conceptual analysis' or 'ordinary-language philosophy'. The exponents of this method, assuming as I have done that the speculative ventures of philosophy are always mistakes, diagnose the error involved in them as 'mistaking the logic of our language', or some such offence against the propriety of the common tongue in which all our communication proceeds. This diagnosis has surprised many people, but it should not surprise us. Speculative philosophers attend to one set of speech or thought habits alone, and determine rigorously the consequences of taking none but these seriously. Thus, for example, by attending to one aspect of our use of the term 'knowledge' it is possible to demonstrate that no one *really* knows anything; the fact that someone who says 'I don't know' may be deliberately lying is either ignored or relegated to the limbo of vulgar error. The remedy for the distortion that necessarily results from such practices is methodically to extend one's attention equally to the whole range of our habits of speech and thought, and concentrate less on the supposed consequences of some of them than on the actual complexities and interrelations of them all. Such concentration reveals that, as Nietzsche long ago divined, ordinary ways of thinking and talking embody more, finer and subtler distinctions in the field of conduct, and accordingly should combine to provide a fuller and more satisfying image of man, than any of the skeletal monsters devised by speculative thinkers.[17] An image thus composed would necessarily reflect all the nuances of humanity that are forced on our attention in the complex courses of our everyday lives, without the philosopher's privilege of ignoring all that does not suit his isolated reveries.

This constant checking of thought against the complexities of the common moral understanding is reinforced in some quarters, as R. M. Hare has explained in a most revealing article on the teaching of philosophy at Oxford,[18] by a deliberate refusal to allow the speculative momentum to get under way. In order to get inside a philosophical system it is necessary initially to suspend one's disbelief, to make oneself see things the philosopher's way. When the adjustment is made and the viewpoint is familiar, one may then decide whether it will do. But one is in no position to make this decision until one has become acclimatized within the philosophy, which one cannot be unless one first commits oneself to it. This initial act of confidence, according to Hare, the philosophers of Oxford refuse to make, or to allow their students to make. 'If I had not believed,' cried Augustine, 'I should never have understood.' Precisely so, says Hare; and all understanding that demands such a prior act of faith must be self-deception. 'People may habituate themselves to anything, even to the very worst things,' said Tolstoy.[19] By refusing to commit oneself, one can be sure of not becoming accustomed and acclimatized, and so one can be sure of not understanding, and so of not believing. The Oxford philosopher says to every other philosopher 'I don't understand what you mean.' And this is not a confession of failure, but a cry of triumph.

It may seem strange that this philosophy, which proclaims itself the ally of common sense against humbug, should have aroused intense hostility; but it has. I cannot account for the bitterness of the feeling, except that philosophy in its critical aspect has always aroused enmity in those with delusions to protect. But there are at least three objections to its procedures which look as if they may have something in them.

The first objection is that this method of philosophy does nothing but confirm the prejudiced and complacent in their prejudicial complacency: it can detect only the errors of minorities, never those of the majority. Yet majority opinions, as I have remarked, do not necessarily reflect realities, even social realities, rather than the malign fatuities of folklore. The analytic philosophy singles out for attack those systems which claim superiority in refinement and exaltation to those of the vulgar mass; and these are arrogantly assumed to be in error before they are shown to be so. Thus the sophist panders to the whims of the many-headed beast, assuring it that the lion and the man are mere excrescences.[20] The objection seems formidable, amounting to a charge of the basest philistinism. But a recollection of our previous arguments suggests that it rests on a mere misunderstanding. First, the analytic philosophy does not confirm the opinions that the man in the street holds but explores the distinctions that he makes. The social delusions of which I have spoken belong to the level of rationalization and ideology rather than to this fine structure of practical discourse. Second, so far from being cruder than the refinements of theory, the distinctions made in practice are found to be finer and subtler. Third, the objection assumes that the speculations such philosophy cuts off stand some chance of attaining a higher truth, instead of merely elaborating a prejudice more restrictive than that of the majority. But I have been arguing that they do not stand any such chance, since their procedure is simply to omit and ignore. It is, after all, the image of man and his world that is in question; and here, surely, truth is more likely to follow recursive catholicity than extrapolative abstraction. 'All the ladders start in the foul rag-and-bone shop of the heart.'

The second objection to analytic philosophy is like the first, namely that it denies the possibility of removing error through scientific discovery, since the scientist must necessarily depart from 'common sense' and does not use 'ordinary language'. But this objection is a complete mistake, though Russell kept making it. The sciences, even the social sciences, are nondeliberative, designed to secure ever more and better facts and explanations in a context that is initially restricted, not at all to evaluate these contexts themselves and decide how men and their world should on the whole be thought of. An 'ordinary-language' philosopher has nothing to say to scientists, except insofar as they suppose, as they sometimes do, that their researches have imposed as necessary a certain view of man and his world, instead of contributing data for possible views. For any scientist is entitled to insist that his facts and theories must not be ignored, but not that they must be given precedence over all others. And surely the sciences must all start from, and in the end all refer to, one world, the world of common experience.[21]

It used to be thought, as Russell thought, and some may still think, that not the world and language of common experience but the purified language and ideal world of mathematics was the clearing-house of all human thought. The belief is understandable. The growth of the sciences has been the growth of mathematical techniques and their application. The scientific revolution was essentially the discovery that by transposing our inquiries into terms of exact quantities we can make their answers testable and mutually interlocking in a way quite impossible to the qualitative and inexact ways of thinking that we usually apply to our everyday concerns. Knowledge in these new terms is so assured and fecund that it is natural to hope for a day when all our thinking will be carried on so. And that mathematics is indeed the most important achievement of the human mind, both in its intrinsic worth and in its significance for our life as a whole, is beyond question. But the practical primacy of calculation as a way of human thought has lately been discredited, as effectively as the camera disproved the practical primacy of representation in painting, by the development of electronic computers. As soon as photography produced closer likenesses than any painter could, everyone realized that producing close likenesses was not what painting was for: since painters had not been replaced and did not feel outdone by photographers, it was evident that their capacities and aims were different. The bluff of an ancient but never tenable thesis had at last been called. Similarly, the very fact that computers, structurally so much simpler than the human brain, can perform mathematical operations more swiftly and accurately than the human mind can, and that the human mind shows no signs of being thrown out of business, has compelled us to recognize that such calculation is not what brains do best and hence presumably not what they are chiefly for. What distinguishes brains from computers, it seems, is their indefiniteness: that, because of the minuteness of their structure, they receive and store information in huge amounts, and for practical purposes as continua rather than as sums of discrete impulses; and that, in consequence, human minds are very flexible, and good at producing unexpected solutions to problems imprecisely formulated. Serendipity, the gift of falling into a sewer and coming up with a gold watch in each hand, is the mark of successful human thinking. Our calculations and quantifications are elaborate and painful constructions on the outskirts of our thought, while our improvisatory skills of organization, integration and just getting along stand unnoticed at the centre. But the reason why we do not notice them is just that they are always there and cause no trouble.

It is only in the last twenty years that computers and the theory of their construction and use have come downstage on the intellectual scene; and it is no coincidence that it is just in this time of the triumph of calculation that writers on the philosophy of science have begun to lose interest in the mathematical structure of scientific theories, their computer-like aspects, and turned their attention to the originality, spontaneity and creativity of scientific discovery. And I should not be surprised to see, in the next few years, a rehabilitation in the intellectual world of the informal and discursive procedures of philosophy and the humane studies generally, which have so long received the hypocritical reverence that longevity commands rather than the practical respect accorded to wage-earners. Be that as it may, the second objection to 'ordinary-language' philosophy, that it is anti-scientific and sub-mathematical, has turned out to rest both on a questionable doctrine about the status of mathematics and on a failure to grasp the distinction between factual and deliberative inquiries.

The third objection to this way of philosophizing is more telling, though it is less often stated explicitly than evinced in the attitudes of its critics. It is, that the claim to a privileged place within the sanctum of common sense is false. These philosophers show a strange lack of self-knowledge in their belief that their philosophy does not itself demand an initial act of faith, as much as any other. It is notorious that students take as long to acclimatize themselves to this as to any other mode of philosophizing; longer, if anything, since besides being subtle and sophisticated in its methods it rests for its justification on a previous reasoned rejection of more intellectually ambitious philosophies. In districts where no other philosophy is rife, this need for indoctrination can escape notice, for students indoctrinate each other; but in less favoured climes it is all too evident. Contrary to what Hare seems to think, it comes easy to the human mind, if not slothful, to be speculative; it is the more restrained and disciplined forms of mental activity that are hardest to learn. Whatever good reasons for such philosophizing there may be, the preservation of the young mind's pristine virginity cannot be one of them.

If Hare is wrong in thinking that the methods of 'ordinary-language' philosophy recommend themselves immediately to common sense without the prior act of faith required to adopt the necessary viewpoint, he is just as innocently mistaken in supposing that the need for acclimatization would constitute an objection to a philosophy. All learning involves habituation; and this applies no more to intellectual disciplines than to manual skills and to social situations. One has to 'settle down' in a new job, a new country, a new house, or a new philosophy before one can operate successfully within it. There is always a period at first in which one must peg away without encouragement, in blind confidence that sooner or later one will begin to feel at home.

It seems, then, that so far as remoteness from everyday familiar considerations goes the philosophy of conceptual analysis is just one philosophy among others. Its precautions have not sufficed to save it from the speculative momentum. But why not? How did it get started down the slippery slope? The answer may be learned from the experience of Socrates, who applied methods like those of the conceptual analysts to preoccupations like those of the existentialists. Socrates sought to bring his victims to self-knowledge by helping them to clarify and verbalize the foundations of their own character and behaviour. But to clarify what is confused is to change it into something quite different, for nothing is more characteristic of a thing than the order which it has. So the end of Socrates' endeavours, as Plato saw, was not to reveal the nature of human virtue, and hence of man, but to call into being a new kind of intellectualized virtue, a new kind of rational man. A man cannot achieve self-knowledge, because the nature of his unknown self depends on its being unknown. What he comes to know of himself is always something that he never was before. Similarly, the conceptual order that the analysts discover in the subtle intricacies of 'ordinary language' is an order that it never had before, as is shown by the ease with which parodists can extract humorous alternative structures from the resources of the same common speech.

The paradoxical result of the Socratic inquisition forces on our attention a conclusion which our argument has long demanded, but which I have been reluctant to draw: that *any* kind of conceptualization must be false to the nature of human experience. 'Man is—what we all know', and this knowledge that we all have is not something that can be summarized and stated, but the whole of our experience. No philosophy can enshrine this knowledge unless it is a philosophy without concepts. One might suppose that there could be no such thing; but it is in fact to such a philosophy that Jaspers urges us to resort. Such a philosophy, of course, could not be spoken or written, but only spoken or written *about*. The house of unperverted thought is a tower of silence. Jaspers accepts this: his voluminous works are, he insists, not philosophy, but ways of arousing in their reader a philosophy which must remain for ever inarticulate.[22]

I have touched here on a pervasive theme of modern thought, one that turns up in many places in many guises—in the methodological doubts of experimental psychology and cultural anthropology, in the anti-intellectualism of modern movements in art, and, as the principle of indeterminacy, even in physics: namely, that observation itself always disturbs what is observed. The remedy in philosophy would seem to be that offered by the more fashionable varieties of what passes in the West for oriental philosophy: to confine one's philosophy to an oblique glance that will not disturb its object as a direct gaze would. The basic feeling is old and pre-philosophical, and is symbolized in that most haunting of childhood games, 'grandmother's footsteps'. In this game, one child turns his back while his playfellows sneak up on him, freezing instantly as their victim whirls around to catch them, if he can, in motion. The same theme is to be found in all those fairy tales in which the furniture talks and dances while the family is asleep; for the converse of the belief that observation fixes is that non-observation releases. The great appeal of Kant's 'Copernican revolution' in philosophy was that it carried this fairy-tale theme to the highest level. Kant taught us to accept as ultimate and irreducible the distinction between man as he observes himself to be but really is not and man as as he really is but cannot observe himself to be. This absolves us from the need for anxious squinting and peering.

Not all philosophers have accepted Kant's heroic renunciation of the elusive self-knowledge. Bergson, for one, thought that in artistic intuition one could have a knowledge of human life which escaped the distorting effects of schematizing intellect and categorizing language, just as certain followers of Heracleitus thought that one might obtain an undisturbed awareness of the ever-changing world simply by refusing to talk about it.[23] But Bergson's device fails no less than that of the conceptual analysts. What he hopes for as the result of abjuring intellectualization is a 'world' of bare uninterpreted perception and feeling; and this is supposed to be the fundamental, undisguised reality of human experience. But in reality neither the artist nor anyone else can find in his experience any such uninterpreted percepts.[24] What is thus put forward as natural and real turns out to be a construction as unreal and abstract as the most sophisticated schematizations of the intellect. All our experience comes to us as meaningful, as interpreted; and it is idle to call such directly inherent meanings and interpretations distortions, when the supposed reality which they are alleged to distort is something which one can only catch a glimpse of, if at all, by elaborate efforts. And if a faithful knowledge of reality is to be strenuously won, why should it be by these efforts rather than any others? Bergson's solution, which is philosophy's last resort in its struggle to escape self-reflection, is no more successful than any of the others. In straining to achieve an undistorted truth it succeeds, like all the rest, only in developing the consequences of taking up a particular stance.

So in the end it appears that there is no mirror in which man may see either his own face; or, like the astronomer, the universe around him; or, like the submarine commander and the searchlight crew, his goal; or, like the person in the crowd, his invisible King;—undistorted by the reflecting medium. Apparently philosophers can discover, not what it is to be human, but only what it is like to be one or another kind of philosopher. Well, never mind. If man is what we all know, we do not depend on philosophy to get us this knowledge. I conclude that if the aim of philosophy is the knowledge of humanity, the best way to philosophize is to stop philosophizing.

That conclusion really will not do. The inarticulate 'knowledge' of humanity that we have by being human is no kind of philosophy at all, let alone the best kind. Besides, if it is true that self-knowledge changes the known self, it is no less true that the changed self is every bit as real as the unchanged. Changing a man, as Socrates protested, is not the same as killing him,[25] and there is no reason why the alteration should be for the worse. The effect of the suggestion that all reflection should be rejected as falsification is to allot a preferential position, as paradigm of humanity, to men who never wonder about themselves. To me, this seems a strange preference.

Perhaps what it is like to be a philosopher may be something worth knowing, after all. It is some comfort to recollect that when the queen in the story asked

> *Mirror, mirror on the wall,*
> *Who is the fairest one of all?*

she got the answer 'you are' only because she, in fact, was. Some, like Plato, would take a strong line about this: they would boldly march whither their fate would drag them and roundly declare that the most significant fact about man is that his mind ranges freely. To such thinkers, man-as-intellectual is the most significant kind of man in the cosmic economy, the missing link between ape and angel; and the fact that philosophy is itself the architect of the humanity that it discovers is not philosophy's shame but its chief justification. It is more fashionable, however, to offer a more modest version of the same defence. *Of course*, one says, it is only as philosopher that man can know himself: to ask, even by implication, those portentous questions 'What is man?' and 'What shall man be?' is already to philosophize. But, one then goes on to say, to refrain from asking these questions is to renounce freedom and decision, to abjure the very task of being human. The questions that philosophers ask are only more articulate versions of those that all men ask, and the asking of which constitutes their humanity. Philosophy's reflexive, deliberative task is to keep man human, to ensure that he continues to know himself as a deliberative animal, as Hare and Sartre unite in urging: the being who is able, by 'self-knowledge', to change the 'self' that he knows.

If that more modest apologia be accepted, what I said at the beginning was philosophy's first question, 'What is philosophy?', is not really different from its last question, 'What are man and his world?'. To ask how we should philosophize is already to ask what we shall make of ourselves. Both are deliberative questions, to which no answer can ever be definitive, although some answers are worse than others and some will never do at all. But if that be true, if a philosopher in saying what man is can reveal nothing but the implications of his own activity as inquirer, it may be equally true that in this essay I have not told you what philosophy is but only what I am going to make of philosophy, or what philosophy must be shown to be by a discourse organized as this one has been. In fact, like all who enter a hall of mirrors, we have only succeeded in losing ourselves thoroughly.

That really is the end of that. The conclusion reached in 'The
Central Problem of Philosophy' has been generalized to the whole
scope of philosophy and has brought our quest to a definite end.
If we continue, we do so because we can generalize yet further,
beyond the range of philosophy itself, and thus return our discussion
whence it began in the general commerce of civilized discourse.
So we end as we started, in dialogue, with the philosopher's voice
one among others, responding to and shaped by other voices no
less shrill than his own.

In thrusting philosophy back into the river of life we encounter a
paradox, which is nothing but our old paradox in a new form. Just
as before we had to say that involvement precluded truth, but only
truth deserved and demanded involvement, so now we have to
admit that philosophy apart from the world is meaningless, but
philosophy in the world must dissipate itself The principle involved
here was perhaps discovered and has certainly been most
systematically studied by McLuhan:[1] concentration varies inversely
with involvement. It is the things that one cares most deeply for
that one is casual about; what receives close attention is by that very
act sealed off from the stream of living.

The dilemma that thus recurs to plague us has the same form as
that which has teased theorists of the drama in all ages: if one
believes that what passes onstage is 'real', one loses the play and
misses the point; if one remains conscious that all is pretence, the
play cannot grip. Five solutions to this dilemma have been
traditionally favoured: to embrace full empathy; to renounce

empathy altogether; to find an appropriate middle position of 'aesthetic distance'; to oscillate between the two poles of belief and disbelief; and to reject the polarity as irrelevant, in that the question of believing or disbelieving does not arise at all, since the players are not pretending but acting. The last solution, that of Coleridge,[2] seems plainly the best. But it gives no obvious clue to the analogous puzzle of philosophical involvement. Certainly the fusion of subhuman (or superhuman) insight with human critique rules out the analogues of the first two solutions, which we may call the barnstorming and the Brechtian. Some tension, or balance, or compromise, or dialectical sublimation of the polarity must be sought. But perhaps there are as many solutions to the predicament as there are philosophers.

It may be that in 'Franciscus' we were after all wrong to dodge the question 'what is a question?' For the axiom that a philosopher's task is to question everything may be taken in three ways. First, it may be his task to call everything into existential doubt, a doubt that he himself feels as a man. Second, his task may be to call everything into a serious methodological doubt that is yet not existential, that he adopts merely as a basis for his philosophizing without letting it affect his unprofessional hours. Third, his task may be to go through the motions of doubting, to raise merely for form's sake the fundamental questions whose answers are never really in doubt at all, before getting on to the serious business of expounding and developing dogma. All of these ways of philosophizing have been tried. And which way, we may well ask now, which way has this book been taking?

But that is the question whose answer we said at the very beginning could never be answered within the work about which it was raised.

Among the voices with which the voice of philosophy holds its conversation is that of poetry. Francis, the anti-philosopher, who in 'Franciscus' related philosophy through its form to the word-play of riddling, now relates it through its dialectic to the word-play of poetry. It is in poetry that the posing and resolution of this book's dilemma has been most familiar, that it has been most recognized that self-expression is self-discovery and self-discovery is self-making, that personal outcry issues in objectivity. The resolution is simple. The workings of original composition, it is argued, are unconscious; necessarily so, because what comes to consciousness is already finished and definite. And what is unconscious is subhuman. It is the critical activity, accepting and moulding what is thus spewed up, that is truly human, and that humanizes the anarchic mass of the dark soul. As a Greek father conferred humanity on his child by taking him into his arms before the hearth and thus receiving him into family and city, so the critical mind makes itself and its works human by accepting and arranging them. Even a computer can be made to write poems by throwing out sequences of lines composed by set rules; but what makes the product poetry is the recognition, selection and arrangement of this material by the machine's human master. At the outset of this inquiry I asked: 'Must we for ever be explaining, and explaining, and explaining? Especially as our explanations are usually wrong.' Now we see that our explanations are necessarily wrong, but wrong only in transcending the vegetable. It is in the falsification that we show ourselves human.

Everyone now admits, and the next dialogue explores the theme, that the tension of creation and criticism and the unaccountability of the originative processes of the mind pervade all forms of independent intellectual activity. If 'Xanthippe' concentrates on poetry, that is not only because it is in fact in connection with poetry that the issue has been most discussed. It is also because in moving towards an account of philosophy as having to do with the limits of the knowable and hence of the sayable—an account traditional enough in itself—the argument has in effect moved towards an approximation of philosophy to poetry. This approximation must now be reckoned with and to some extent neutralized. Thus, as I remarked before, Francis the anti-philosopher who first assumed the guise of a riddler now assumes that of a poet. It is the poet who cannot acquiesce in any restriction on what may be said or whistled, whose essential business is with what plain prose cannot achieve, and whose interests are served by some of the interpretations and tendencies of the argument of this book.

That the literary responsibilities of poetry and philosophy are complementary I have already said. A closer connection was suggested by Collingwood: 'Quite otherwise than the scientist, and far more than the historian, the philosopher must go to school with the poets in order to learn the use of language, and must use it in their way: as a means of exploring one's own mind, and bringing to light what is obscure and doubtful in it.'[3] But philosophers are to poets, he adds, as lens-grinders are to jewellers: their art must conceal itself.

I have argued that a difference in method argues a difference of aim. So perhaps the likeness of method that Collingwood alleges argues a likeness of aim. Poetry, I have suggested, may be a continuation of philosophy by other means. Both are branches of literature, modes of ordered discourse designed to organize a more or less intractable experience. And it is possible that the criteria of success in philosophy and poetry may be more alike in practice than they are generally admitted to be, for philosophy in our day has become so caught up in the academic machine that its vital relation to the realities of human intercourse has been obscured. Those who take part in the ceremony of Kissing the Backside of the Ph.D. Octopus do well not to invite scrutiny of their postures, and it is considered unprofessional as well as unconventional to look into the more general implications of philosophical methods. But the rest of us may still fix these ungainlinesses with our roving glance.

Xanthippe

My friends tell me I am too old, but I say that you are as young as you feel, so here I was in my old khaki drill shorts canoeing up the river after an early start. It would be hot, and by the time I reached the mouth of the Cherwell at mid-morning I had come far enough for the day; so I turned up that shadowy water with the idea of a lazy afternoon after a little book-shopping.

It was about tea-time when I was smoking a pipe in the meadow below Marston Ferry and watching the shipping on the river. A punt came upstream with two female passengers, slowly propelled by a youngish, tallish, baldish man who wore one of the all-overish beards that used to be affected in those days by persons who liked to feel rebellious without actually rebelling. The girl in the bow had carroty hair, somewhat darker at the scalp, green ear-rings like unripe pears, a sort of crimson sort of blouse thing, peacock-blue matador pants, and paint everywhere. Surely, I thought, that can only be—

She saw me. She waved her hankie. She screeched: 'Eeeeh! Xenny! Xenny boy!'

The man on the pole turned to see what was occasioning this demonstration. That was his mistake. His neglected pole trailed outward, the stern of the punt swung in, a willow stump caught him above the knees and he sank noisily. Oh, well, I thought, it happens all the time. I gave him a hand out and lent him my raincoat while he got his clothes dried. Meanwhile the girls had retrieved the pole and paddled their craft to land. I helped them make the punt fast and they came ashore. 'Hello, Xanthippe,' I said, 'what have you done with Socrates?'

'He'll be along for tea, he's coming overland with that dreadful What's-his-name, *you* know, man used to be his secretary.'

'Oh yes, I know, what *was* his name? I didn't know he'd left Socrates.'

'Yes, he's on his own now, *very* big man, but he still likes to have Siggy hanging around, can't think why unless it's his way of showing off.'

'And who—?'

'Oh, *so* sorry. Kitty dear, this is Major Xenophon, or is it Colonel, one of Siggy's very oldest friends, haven't seen him for *ages*, fights in the oddest armies, *such* a romantic man. Xenny, Kitty Sparshott, *sweet* girl, comes from Montreal, you've met her husband.'

'Of course yes, long time ago, didn't recognize him. How do you do, Mrs. Sparshott. Charmed.'

'How do you do.'

So while they organized their paraphernalia I talked to my old acquaintance, now shivering and looking vinegarish under my waterproof while his clothes dried in the sun. 'Hello, Francis, I didn't know you.'

'Hello.'

'What are you doing now?'

'Teaching philosophy.'

'How do you like it?'

'It's a job.'

'How long have you been married?'

'Years.'

'Where are you teaching?'

'Toronto.'

'How do you like it?'

'It's a place.'

'Well, Socrates was right. I remember in the old days, he always used to say, "That boy will go far," he said.'

'Oh.'

My fault. I should have remembered that jokers don't like others to make jokes. So I created a diversion. 'Anyone read any good books lately?' I asked, throwing it out to the group as they say.

'Why yes,' said Xanthippe, 'just *too* instructive, *all* about how poets write poems. You have no idea. I always thought they just went and wrote, but it seems there's a regular *process*.'

'The creative process?' suggested Kitty.

'Why you *clever* girl. Sounds just like something that happens in cheese, doesn't it, I mean *it*, not *you*, darling. Well, what happens is, something happens to this poet that makes him suffer *terribly*, it must be *awful* being a poet, so he starts turning it into a poem so that it won't feel so bad, only after a bit he gets stuck, but the poem doesn't, it goes right *deep* down into his unconscious and keeps churning and churning around and gets hooked up with all kinds of other junk down there until *in* the end it comes back up all of a sudden and he finds he's finished his poem without knowing it and feels *lots* better.'

'Jesus Murphy!' said Kitty. 'Who wrote that stuff? Robert Graves?'

'Livingston Lowes?' I guessed.[1]

'Could be anyone,' said Francis gloomily. 'Romantic orthodoxy. It still goes on.'

'Oh,' said Xanthippe, 'some *man* wrote it.'

'Isn't that how you write your poems, Francis?' said Kitty.

'Good gracious, Francis,' I said, 'I didn't know you were a poet. Why don't you publish?'

'I do, in Canadian magazines.'

'I mean, publish properly, in England.'

There didn't seem to be a suitable answer to that one, so Francis went back to his wife's enquiry. 'You don't have to wait for something to distress you before you can start,' he said. 'It may be just an idea for a poem. But it's quite true that there's often a period of unconscious incubation before you can finish. And sometimes the whole poem does seem to be given to you, all at once, and you don't know what you've done until you look at it afterwards.'

"Well you know,' I said, 'that bit doesn't sound too different from writing philosophy. You feel preoccupied, but you aren't actually thinking about anything, more like waiting.'

'For the angel to trouble the waters?' said Xanthippe.

'Waiting, anyway. Then quite suddenly the whole thing falls into place, or a great chunk of it does, and all you have to do is write it out.'

'Yes,' said Francis, 'so far as the writing goes, it's really very much the same sort of thing.'

'Ha, interesting,' boomed a voice behind me. 'Most interesting.' I turned, and there was Socrates' former secretary, looming down at us with a genial glare.

How he had changed. He was looking much bigger, and burlier, and grizzled and furrowed about the brows, and his bare forearms and toes (for he wore sandals) were sparsely grown with rank black hairs; and he had acquired a masterful crouching stoop. On his starboard quarter, Socrates, the same as ever, was bobbing and beaming, like Mary's little lamb. Introductions and sounds of reunion.

'I heard what you were saying,' said the secretary—we never did remember his name, which had cramped the introductions somewhat. 'Now, what does this likeness you were talking about come right down to? Come on, chaps, sharpen up a bit.'

Francis must have been used to the man's manner, for he answered without protest: 'Well, for one thing, after I've got an idea of what I want to write and before I write it there's often a sort of dead period, when I'm lethargic and moody and irritable, and can't settle down to anything. It feels as if I'm waiting for something to happen. Perhaps I may worry over bits of what I have to do, but I can't bring myself really to get down to thinking about it.'

I recognized the symptoms. 'Quite so. You sort of shrink into yourself and can't bear to concentrate on anything, as though it were important to keep your mind quiet. Most odd feeling.'

'I don't know that I'd put it that strongly, but that's the kind of thing, yes, and it's the same whether you're writing a poem or an article.'

'All right,' said the secretary, 'feeling of inertia. Anything else? That isn't much.'

'Yes, then there's the way the work comes out at the end of this dead period. It comes quite rapidly and without further reflection, and sometimes the results are quite unforeseen. I mean, quite complex stanzas and orderly chains of argument may appear as if ready made. There they are, and you see that they're characteristic of you, but it doesn't seem as if you were responsible for them.'

'It must save you a lot of trouble,' said Kitty, 'to have an Unconscious to do your thinking for you. Pity you can't teach it to type, or would you have to pay it?'

'But what could be simpler?' said Xanthippe. 'You know what the Unconscious uses for money. *All* you'd have to do—'

'Yes, yes, yes,' said Francis. 'What rich little minds you girls have. Well, the next thing is, that any work that's done like this is awfully hard to revise. You can tinker with it, but you can't get it into focus properly. It's as hard to see clearly afterwards what you've done as it was to think about it systematically beforehand. The result is that I can pass work that's full of awkwardnesses and absurdities that I should immediately spot and condemn in anyone else's writing.'

'Just a minute,' said Socrates. 'You say your work is full of undetected errors. How do you know?'

'Well, I mean, they're obvious.'

'You detect your undetected errors? Then—'

'Not at once. Sometimes I do after a while, but usually some kind friend shows me. As soon as they're pointed out, they're obvious, and I can't imagine how I came to pass them. As if something got between me and them, and now it got out of the road.'

'I see,' said the secretary. 'Instantaneous composition, and inability to bring attention to bear. That makes three. Any more?'

'The only other thing I can think of is that when I'm doing anything on a big scale, prose or verse, ideas for smaller works in the same medium often pop up in my mind, as if they were by-products.'

'You mean lyrics are chips off epics?' said Xanthippe. 'My dear, how *thrilling*. Churning away was right.'

'Eh?'

'*You* know, the *poem*, dear, churning away under the surface there, just like my good book said.'

'Oh, the book.'

'Good!' said the secretary, briskly; 'Fourth point: generalized creative ferment. Right? Right. Anything more? Nothing more. I see. Fair enough, you've convinced me.'

'What of? I didn't know anyone was proving anything,' said Francis.

'You have persuaded me that, from the subjective point of view, the processes of writing are much the same whether it is prose or verse that is in question. Or at least, that they are sufficiently alike for the identity of the process to be assumed as an hypothesis. Now, what interested me in your comparison was this. I don't know if any of you have ever heard of anything called the "creative process" or sometimes the "poetic process"—'

'Don't worry, old chap, we all know all about it,' I said.

'You've been reading one of Xanthippe's good books, that's what you've been doing,' said Francis gloomily.

'Perhaps I may have. Anyway, I have made some study of the literature of the subject, and I find that from the lack of conscious continuity between inception and completion of a poetic work certain inferences are sometimes drawn. And it occurred to me that if this discontinuity is no less characteristic of philosophical composition, as you appear to suggest, these same inferences must also be made in respect of philosophy.'

'What deathless prose you do talk, to be sure,' I said.

'You mean lifeless,' said Francis.

'No doubt my attempt to achieve a degree of precision in utterance lends my speech a certain formality. You must forgive me.'

'Carry right on, we love it. What are these inferences of yours, anyway?'

'There are three of them. The first is, that the statements of which poems consist are not genuine statements. Since the poet is not their conscious author he cannot really be taken as asserting them, and obviously no one else can. Consequently, since no one asserts it, a poem is not real speech but a speech-like artefact, and consists of a "virtual discourse" that is neither true nor false.'

'But surely,' said Francis, 'it isn't just the nature of the processes that end in poems that makes people talk about "virtual discourse." The phrase comes from Mrs. Langer, doesn't it?[2] And she certainly—'

'There may be other reasons. But the inference is made. And what happens if we apply it to philosophy?'

'Obviously,' I said, 'it will follow that philosophy consists of pseudo-statements. Nothing new in that. People are always saying that things philosophers say are pseudo-statements, and neither true nor false but meaningless.'

'Nonsense!' said Francis. 'For one thing, the people who say it are always philosophers, and it's in their philosophy that they say it. And they don't say it about everything every philosopher says in his philosophy—not about what they are saying themselves, for example. They say it of particular utterances that they take to be logically defective because they are neither analytic nor verifiable. To say that all philosophical utterances were pseudo-statements, just because they figured in a philosophical work, would be a new form of extravagance.'

'I dare say you are right,' I rejoined, 'but maybe it's an extravagance we ought to commit. It's all very well to say that what makes pseudo-statements pseudo is not their context but their character, but doesn't meaning depend very largely on context? And if it does I should suppose that meaningfulness does too. I've often thought that maybe after all philosophy is really just a complex kind of rhetoric, whose real value has to be judged by some rhetorical standard, effectiveness or something. I know there are logical criteria for evaluating philosophical arguments. Of course there are. But are they really what we evaluate philosophy by? And anyway, aren't they often just aesthetic tests in disguise, like the elegance of a mathematical demonstration? Cogent arguments are ones that make you want to believe them.'

'Oh, come now, Captain,' said the secretary. 'The sole aim of philosophy is to effect a rational persuasion. You cannot make me think otherwise. It is the rationality that is important. A philosopher who relies on persuasive fallacies is not worthy of the name. A cogent argument is one to which the mind must assent so long as it thinks correctly and rationally.'

'True enough,' said Francis, 'but Xenophon does have a point after all. Otherwise the greatest philosophers and the most convincing philosophers would be the same. But they aren't, you know. Even if you thought that C. D. Broad was almost always right and Plotinus almost always wrong, I expect you would still think Plotinus was the greater philosopher. Look at it this way. Who do you think was the greatest philosopher who ever lived?'

The secretary thought for a moment. 'Hegel,' he said.

'All right. And do you agree with every word that Hegel ever wrote?'

'I cannot honestly say that I do.'

'But when you disagree with him you must think that you are right and he is wrong, or you would change your mind.'

'That is true.'

'And do you think that you are a greater philosopher than Hegel, the "greatest philosopher who ever lived"?'

'Of course not.'

'Then you don't really think that philosophical greatness is the same as correctness of thought.'

'But he argues far more skilfully than I.'

'You said yourself that persuasive fallacies are unworthy of philosophy. And a skilful argument to which you refuse assent must be a persuasive fallacy, unless you are just being pig-headed.'

'Say what you please, you will never convince me that it is inappropriate to ask whether what a philosopher says is meaningful, true and soundly argued. I find your anti-intellectualism deplorable in one who claims to be a philosopher. You have been too long away from the centres of civilization.'

Seeing that Francis was beginning to lose his temper, which I am afraid he was rather apt to when crossed in argument in the days when I knew him, Socrates intervened. 'Just a minute,' he said. 'If I am not mistaken, we are impelled to draw these regrettable conclusions only by analogy with an inference made about poetry. Is that inference itself correct?'

'I really cannot say,' said the secretary, 'I found it in the literature.'

'Ah. Now, was not that inference made from the circumstances in which certain writings were produced?'

'Yes.'

'How can one infer the logical character of a statement from the circumstances of its production?'

'You can't,' said Francis, 'or there would be no such thing as formal logic.'

'In that case you won't mind my saying that I don't really see how this talk about pseudo-statements arises.'

'It's not the logical character of the statements that is in question, Socrates,' I said, 'but their status as serious expressions of opinion as opposed to mere works of art.'

'I see. But surely the question of how a statement was produced is not the same as the question of how it is to be taken?'

'I don't see why not.'

'Suppose you were asked to sign a petition. The wording would not be yours, but by signing it you would be acknowledging as your own the opinions it expressed. Perhaps what you put your name to would be something you never thought of saying yourself. Even so, your endorsement would make the words yours, wouldn't it?'

'I suppose so.'

'Why else would people sign things? But then it doesn't matter how philosophy is composed. The philosopher isn't entranced when he copies it out, signs and publishes it, is he?'

'No.'

'And surely by doing so in full awareness he acknowledges it for his own?'

'It seems so.'

'Then I think my old friends are becoming needlessly embroiled. Neither the logical character of a discourse nor the proper way of taking it is in the least affected by the way it is produced, whether it be verse or prose.'

'But supposing,' I said, 'you were to produce a "poem" by combining at random words taken from a dictionary?'

'Well,' said Francis, 'suppose you did. If you published it as poetry, that would show you meant it to be taken as poetry. The only question would be whether it was any good. Of course it would be most unlikely to be a good poem, produced that way, but it's not absolutely impossible. After all, it wouldn't be any good anyway, if you were writing it.'

'But people are always doing it, for a hoax.'

'It's a hoax that cannot succeed. The intention is to show that editors can't tell good verse from bad. But if the people the hoax is meant to impress need to be told how the verse was produced, that proves that they can't tell good verse from bad either. So the whole silly business is absolutely pointless.'

There was a pause while we got on with the tea the girls had been handing out. I have been simplifying my report of the conversation by leaving out remarks like 'Cucumber sandwich?' and by not trying to reproduce the indistinctness of utterance produced by full mouths, but we had been eating steadily and now ate more steadily yet.

I broke the comparative silence by saying: 'That seems to tie up one of the inferences, anyway.'

'What inferences?' said Kitty. 'You lost me.'

'Inferences from lack of conscious continuity between starting and finishing writing. Weren't there two others?'

'There were indeed,' said the secretary, hastily swallowing a mouthful of cake so as not to miss his opportunity. 'The second one is this. Because it is the unconscious mind that produces the poem, it is supposed that a poem is no mere artefact but rather an extension, so to say, of the poet's suffering self: an expression of his emotion.'

'I don't see the connection,' I said.

'The nerve of the inference is, I take it, that on the one hand the poet has expended little conscious labour on his poem, and on the other hand the discoveries of the late Dr. Freud require us to regard everything that takes place in the unconscious mind as intimately bound up with the ultimate determinants of our character and conduct.'

'Yes,' said Xanthippe, 'and it's *most* unfair. After all the hard work I put in on my poor outside, people go around saying that isn't the real me, the real me's way down inside where I can't get at it. Ungrateful beasts, I *hate* them.'

'Never mind them, Xanthippe,' said Francis, 'just keep right on putting a good face on things. He can't have it both ways. First he says a poem's an artefact because the poet didn't mean it, now he says it isn't an artefact because the poet did mean it. Make up your mind, chum.'

'I have already told you that I am merely reporting what I find in the literature.'

'I don't see the inconsistency, Francis,' I said. 'To be an expression of opinion the work would have to be consciously intended, which it isn't. To be an expression of deep feeling it has to be unconsciously determined, which it is.'

'All right, all right, I apologize.'

'I'm sure Francis' philosophy expresses his emotion, the way he groans about it,' said Kitty. 'When he's thinking he lies awake all night and scratches.'

'What *exciting* lives you lead,' said Xanthippe. 'Siggy *never* has to scratch *his* philosophy, do you, dear? But do tell us, I've always wanted to know but I didn't *dare* ask, how deep down does your philosophy really go?'

'I really don't know, dear,' said Socrates. 'I just try to find out the truth and I never really thought of doing anything else. But then, I never thought of philosophy as something you wrote. I used to get into arguments and see where they led, and if they led to any conclusion I believed that until a better argument showed me I was wrong.'

'Yes, Socrates,' I said, 'but we can't all be like you. You're conscious all the way down. Most of us take up positions and defend them. If we lose, we don't change our opinions; we look for better arguments to support our old convictions. Seems as if we're more deeply committed to the views we happen to hold than we are to the job of reaching the truth. If we were purely dispassionate reasoners, arguments we proposed would mean no more to us than arguments other men proposed. There's no real room for taking sides in a scientific enquiry.'

'Francis gets furious when he reads his reviews,' said Kitty.

'I'm afraid I do rather,' said Francis, 'though I should like to think that what annoys me is that people can't be bothered to read what one has written.'

'Perhaps you don't write very clearly,' said the secretary.

'I suppose that may be it. But what's really interesting is to see a group of philosophers arguing. Quite often a man begins by defending a subtle and elaborate thesis, but gets tired after a while and ends by just affirming and re-affirming some quite crude dogma. Then you can see that the subtle thesis was just the dogma dressed up. I've seen disputants so obsessed that they couldn't see the force of quite decisive points. They just don't seem to hear the fatal remarks. Like chickens running round with their heads cut off. That happens even to mathematical logicians, and you'd think if anything was purely rational and impersonal that would be.'

'Would it be your opinion,' said the secretary, 'that these lapses from rationality are occasioned by a mere ego-involvement with one's opinions because one has espoused them as one's own? Or does the content of the opinion itself reflect the deeper levels of the personality, as Nietzsche maintained?'[3]

'Why, you *short*-memoried old thing, you!' said Xanthippe. 'Don't you remember, Francis does *all* his philosophy in his little unconscious while the rest of him's asleep or falling in the river or something. Which reminds me, Francis, *do* put your trousers back on, you look *most* ungainly, doesn't he, Kitty? But I suppose you're used to it. *Anyway*, what I mean is, if Francis' opinions *don't* reflect his deeper levels they're missing a perfectly *marvellous* opportunity.'

During these revelations Socrates had been looking first puzzled, then deeply distressed, and finally very abstracted and thoughtful. Now he said: 'These philosophers who don't change their minds when defeated in argument. Would these opinions they revert to be ones they've discussed before?'

'I suppose so,' I said.

'It seems likely, if they're so fond of them. But if that is so they must surely have become familiar with very many arguments for and against them.'

'One would think so.'

'After all, they must be difficult and complicated questions, or they wouldn't keep arguing about them.'

'No, there must be two arguable sides to them.'

'Then shouldn't we suppose that the opinions to which these men cling are those which the arguments they know tend *on the whole* to support?'

'One would like to think so.'

'Like it or not, it seems probable. And if so, I don't see why it's so irrational for them to decline to change their opinions at short notice. Wouldn't a man say, "Well, those arguments go against my position, but I know there are a lot of others in my favour, only I just can't put my tongue to them at the moment"? I'm very ignorant myself, as you know, but I imagine that people with a lot of knowledge must often find it hard to turn up the bit they want. They'd be like Xanthippe with her hand-bag, which is always full of things, and she has to rummage for a long time before she finds what she wants, and quite often she can't find it at all until it's too late, can you, my dear?'

But Xanthippe was listening to Kitty explaining how easy it was to bake one's own bread, and did not hear.

'That's all very well,' I said, 'but Francis mentioned a lot of other facts you haven't explained away yet.'

'You young people talk so fast,' said Socrates. 'I can only think of one thing at a time.'

'Surely,' said the secretary, 'not all philosophers are so wrapped up in their work as that? There must be some who are quite reasonable, and go about their tasks methodically.'

'Of course,' said Francis. 'Socrates does, for one. But some poets are quite rational and systematic, too, so my analogy doesn't break down there. Now, how about the third of your inferences?'

'Ah yes,' said the secretary. 'If poets produce their poems without thinking about them, it follows that when a critic goes to work on a poem his is the only rational intelligence at work. A poet cannot tell you what his poem means; only a critic can do that, and the poet has no authority to contradict him. My question is accordingly whether analogous reasoning can be applied to philosophy. Is the philosophical critic a rational man dealing with the fruits of unreason?'

'I suppose,' said Kitty, who was taking a few minutes' rest in her exposition to give the dough time to rise, 'that's why we always look at the reviews in the quarterlies first. They're the only sane bits.'

'Reviewers are no saner than anyone else,' said Francis. 'Look at the stuff they write. Can't follow a simple argument. After all, a review is just as much a personal product as a piece of original work is.'

'It just makes me dizzy,'' said Xanthippe, 'to think of all this unconscious incubation going absolutely *incessantly* on. No wonder I have such surly friends. They're all *broody*, every last one of them.'

'Aren't we being a little hasty,' said Socrates, 'in putting the irrationalities we find in reviews and articles down to the effects of unconscious lucubration? I thought Francis said that philosophers were just as unreasonable in conversation as in their writings.'

'That's true,' said Francis.

'But these conversations must have been spontaneous.'

'Yes.'

'Then their unreasonableness can't have been the effect of any unconscious mulling over.'

'The unconscious mind,' said the secretary, 'is alleged never to sleep.'

'Indeed? But if its disturbing effects are equally felt at times of full awareness I fail to see what your third inference is based on. And if unconscious forces do make all philosophers irrational all the time, who is to detect this irrationality? Surely we are not reduced to substituting for the prejudices of others prejudices of our own.'

'No,' I said, 'of course we aren't. There are criteria for arguments and critical techniques, and there are people who can apply them, at least some of the time. Reasons can be adduced and examined. Philosophy really goes on in quite an orderly way, by and large, if you look at the whole picture.'

'I am very glad to hear it. But who are these paragons of sanity?'

'Present company excepted,' said Kitty.

'Why,' said Francis, 'haven't I told you? It's the disinterested by-stander, the onlooker who sees most of the game. The man who is not vitally interested, whose ego is not involved as our friend would say, can keep score. We are all bystanders in more arguments than we are participants in, and that's what keeps the whole thing going. That's why people appeal to posterity. Only those to whom what we're saying doesn't matter any longer can really understand what we say.'

'I don't recall you telling us that,' I said.

'Well, I have now.'

For quite a while after that we smoked and chatted idly, while Francis put on his dry clothes and the girls gathered up the tea-things. Distant traffic growled from the by-pass. The sun still looked as if it meant to shine for ever, but it got lower in the sky. Socrates' former secretary got up and started pacing to and fro, head down, as though looking for cigar-butts. Presently he came back and frowned down at us all. 'I'm not satisfied,' he said.

'You *poor* darling,' said Xanthippe. 'What you need—'

'What does this analogy between poetry and philosophy rest on, anyhow? Just one man's experience. And we all know how Francis gets carried away.'

'Oh, I don't know,' I said. 'This business of the solution to an intellectual problem coming suddenly to mind after the problem has been laid aside isn't at all uncommon. Lord Russell says it happens to him, for one.'[4]

'Yes,' said Francis, 'surely it's quite usual. And that inability to bring oneself to write that I spoke of, that I thought suggested that a writer was deeply involved in his work. Well, that's very common. I imagine we all know lots of people who have work that they badly want to do, and to all appearances are well equipped to do, but simply can not get themselves to the point of actually doing. You find it even with undergraduates writing essays.'

'Surely that's nothing but laziness,' said the secretary.

'You mustn't call my husband lazy,' said Kitty. 'He's always thinking about how he should be working.'

'There's all the difference in the world,' said Francis, 'between this feeling of shrinking from a task, which is quite positive and very uncomfortable, and a mere neglect of one's duties, which is rather pleasant. I can work quite steadily at routine tasks without any blocking at all, if I like, and if I'm not hatching something.'

'Is it anything like putting off an important decision?' said Socrates. 'Some of my friends get very irritable and preoccupied when they're trying to make up their minds about something they'd rather not have to.'

'Yes, I suppose it is rather like that.'

'Then may not the cause of your discomfort be simply that you know you are going to have to commit yourself?'

'You mean, I am putting off as long as possible the dread day when I have to make up my mind what to say? Yes, I suppose that's possible.'

'In that case, while it's true that your writing means a lot to you, we can't take your discomfort as proof that any unconscious processes are under way.'

'I suppose not.'

'And another thing,' I said. 'This inability to see faults in your own work, that you said proved how much it was a part of you. Doesn't that happen with other people's work too? Aren't you often taken in by something that you can see is quite absurd, as soon as someone else points out the absurdity? I know I am.'

'That wasn't quite it,' said Francis. 'It isn't just a failure to notice something, it's a positive feeling that I can't bring attention to bear, as though there were a veil between me and it. I never find that with things other people have written.'

'I'm still worried about this unconscious incubation,' said Socrates. 'Granted you have all these odd feelings, I don't see what they have to do with unconscious processes. As far as I can make out from what you've told us, all you are aware of is the initial posing of a problem and its final solution. So I suppose the unconscious goings on are inferred from something. But I don't see from what.'

'Well,' said Francis, 'there's the suddenness of the solution's coming after the delay, and its unexpectedness, and these feelings of constraint. Something must be going on, and it isn't conscious, so it must be unconscious.'

'Why must something be going on? I thought we agreed that your discomforts could be put down to reluctance to commit yourself.'

'They could, I suppose, but I still don't think they should. And then there's the delay itself.'

'But I don't see why a solution should always occur to one immediately. Surely it does sometimes, and then you don't make any fuss about it. It's like fishing. Sometimes you get a bite at once, sometimes not for hours or not at all. It depends when a fish happens to come along.'

'But then there's the unexpectedness of these complex solutions.'

'Why should they be expected?'

'I don't think I understand.'

'What I mean is, after all, a solution to a problem can't occur to you before it occurs to you, can it?'

'Of course not.'

'Then the first time you think of it, it's bound to be unexpected. How could you have expected it?'

'But it's so sudden, so quick. The whole thing comes at once.'

'Does it? I don't see how you know.'

'Why, all of a sudden there it all is.'

'Not all at once, surely. I don't see how you can know you've got the answer to your problem without going through it. Surely you have to recite the poem to yourself, or write it out, and the same with an argument. And that takes time.'

'But there's a sudden sort of "got it!" feeling when you know you have the solution,' I said.

'I believe I see what Socrates is trying to say,' said the secretary. 'You may *feel* in an instant that you have the solution, but you cannot *know* that you have it in less time than it takes to go through it in your mind. Your sudden feeling might well prove to be mistaken, and would then be ignored when it came to making up your accounts of the processes of composition. Was that not it, Socrates? Though what the relevance of the point is, I confess I am at a loss to say.'

'Thank you, that's it exactly. The point is, you see, that there is nothing strange in a poem or a theory being produced in the time it takes to run through it. Why shouldn't one be able to think with the speed of thought?'

'But they are so complex,' said Francis.

'And why not? Just think how complicated the syntax of an ordinary sentence is, and what a delicate task it is to formulate utterances that will be relevant to what has gone before, interesting to all present, and grievous to the feelings of none. But that's just what we do all the time in an ordinary conversation. We think nothing of it because it happens so often. I doubt if poems and arguments are really more complex than conversations, which we compose with the speed of speech.'

'Surely they have a different kind of complexity.'

'No doubt. But are these instantaneous poems and arguments ever produced by beginners?'

'Not that I ever heard. It only happens to experienced writers, so far as I'm aware.'

'Then surely these are people to whom your "different kind of complexity" has become almost as habitual as that of conversing is to us all. What I'm asking is, why shouldn't a man acquire the knack of rhyming or reasoning as fast as he can talk?—and he can't prove he can do it any faster, can he now? If you think of it, every-thing we do at any instant is instantaneous, and as complicated as its past and future can make it.'

'I suppose that's really the trouble,' I said, 'with all this stuff about creative processes. These accompaniments of composition are things that go on all the time; only when they happen to poets they are thought to be exceptional and significant. All our pains and inspirations are really only interesting to ourselves and our friends. They haven't anything to do with creativity at all.'

'You're both very plausible,' said Francis. 'I can only say that I really do feel as if I were confronted with a structure whose proper-ties I don't immediately understand. I have to look to see what I've done. It isn't *like* writing or talking in the ordinary way.'

'Perhaps not,' said Socrates, 'but why postulate an unconscious process to account for it? Why not just say that some poems and arguments are written very quickly and seem very important to you personally?'

'It isn't just the quickness, it's the lack of volition. Sometimes you sit down deliberately to produce something, but these are things that just come.'

'Doesn't Robert Graves say,' said Kitty, 'that poetry ought to be written like that? I think he says it's wrong to force it—rude to his white goddess, or something.'

'That's right,' said Francis, 'and some Chinese theorists said the same sort of thing about painting.'⁵

'Has anyone ever said that about philosophy, that you ought to wait for the muse to inspire you? That would make a Ph.D. a terribly chancy business, wouldn't it?'

'I should have thought,' said the secretary, 'that one might more credibly affirm the converse. Perhaps philosophers can write as though they were lyric poets, and no doubt your husband does, but I should have expected the result to be bad work. Philosophy surely ought to be a matter of method or routine, as all serious occupations are. Philosophers should not be existentially involved with the content of their theories, and should therefore abjure methods that are associated with such involvement. No doubt such renunciation does not guarantee immunity, but one feels that the effort should be made. In short, there are two ways of writing either philosophy or poetry, and the right way for each is the wrong way for the other.'

'Are you suggesting,' said Socrates, 'that the value of a work depends on the way it was produced? I thought we agreed that its logical character didn't, so I don't see why its worth should either.'

'No, no, Socrates, I was only saying that certain methods tend to produce bad work, not that the method constitutes the demerit.'

'I'm glad to hear it. I was afraid the phrase "creative process" might have led us astray.'

'How so?'

'Well, what do you mean when we call a man "creative"?'

'We mean, I think, that he writes a great deal, if we are speaking of writers, and I take it we are.'

'Don't we mean rather,' I said, 'that his work is original rather than imitative?'

'Now *why* don't you ask little me?' said Xanthippe. 'I actually *took a course* in creative writing once. Siggy was off fighting in Delos or somewhere equally silly and I was so bored I could have screamt. So I took this *exciting*-sounding course, and you know what it was? Fiction. Boy meets girl and all *that* jazz. Original? Ha!'

'Thank you,' said Socrates. 'Whichever of you is right, you see, and I'm sure you all are really, creativeness is a quality of the work done: originality, or abundance, or untruth. Setting a high value on creativity extols a product, not a process. So what does "creative process" mean? It looks as if it ought to mean that process whereby a large quantity of original falsehood is produced, or something like that. But why should there be any such process? A process that guaranteed such abundant originality would indeed be worth knowing for all prospective liars. But as it is, I think the best way to see if something is good is to inspect it, not to ask where it came from.'

'No one is arguing with you about that, Socrates,' I said, 'but I think accounts of how things get done do have a certain interest. Doesn't what we've been saying explain how a great poet like Wordsworth can publish appalling poems, and a great philosopher like Mill can commit blunders that most undergraduates can spot? Critics tend to be condescending about these, as if they were signs of an inflated reputation or something. But it looks as if they're just the inevitable outcome of personal involvement.'

'It takes a Homer to nod like Homer,' said Francis, 'and it is being Homer that makes him nod.'

'Oh, rubbish! It isn't only the great who make silly mistakes. It's just that the surrounding greatness makes them more noticeable.'

'Sorry, I got carried away.'

'Well, now,' said the secretary, 'if poetry and philosophy are not to be distinguished as products of different processes, how are they to be distinguished?'

'*Everyone* knows that, dear,' said Xanthippe. 'Philosophy goes right on to the end of the line, and poetry has too many capital letters, or too few nowadays, *most* confusing for us old-fashioned readers. And you can tell from the prefaces, they're all *terribly* grateful, but poets are grateful to the editor of *Orgasm* and philosophers are grateful to Professor Smith who read the proofs. Besides, you can *tell*. *Honestly*, you ask the *silliest* questions.'

'Yes, my dear, but these differences in form are to a large extent merely traditional. Poets write sonnets because they have read sonnets by other poets, and philosophers thank Professor Smith because other philosophers have thanked Professors Brown and Robinson. I want to know what else determines these differences.'

'You really are being a bit silly, you know,' I said. 'They have quite different jobs. Philosophers try to produce what you call rational conviction in philosophical problems, and poets produce objects for what I'm sure you call aesthetic contemplation.'

'Indeed I do. Why should I not? But I do wish you would be more precise. I take it that you differentiate poetry from philosophy by their ends, and the values they are meant to have. Should we not ask ourselves just what these values are in each case?'

'I don't really see why we should.'

'Because the Professor here has pointed out that the procedures by which poetry and philosophy are produced differ less widely than is popularly supposed. It is equally generally supposed that the standards by which they are to be judged differ yet more widely. I feel that it is incumbent on us to consider the possibility that this supposition may be equally mistaken.'

'Oh, all right, if you say so. What about truth, then? We don't think any the worse of a poet nowadays because we don't think what he says is true. Think of Dante. But no one can suppose that it doesn't matter whether what a philosopher says is true or not.'

'So I should have supposed. But I was told a little while ago that a philosopher's merit does not depend on the truth of his doctrine.'

'So you were,' said Francis. 'And if poets aren't meant to tell the truth, why do people always quote poetry in support of their views? Besides, I'm sure the reason we think so highly of long poems like the *Iliad* is that we feel that there is something satisfying in the view of human affairs they embody. An unsatisfying view may not be quite the same as a false one, but it comes near. We're satisfied because we're made to feel that that's the way things are. And aren't poets supposed to be true to themselves or their vision?'

'Really!' I said. 'You're just playing with words. They should be true to their wives, too, come to that.'

'No, quite seriously, isn't fidelity the essence of truth? I know all about truth not being a property of symbols, and saying "*p* is true" being a way of assenting to *p*, but that stuff only makes sense in a context of formal logic. And surely what we ask of a Kant or a Hume isn't just that their statements should command assent, but that their whole picture of morality or of human knowledge should square with what we know. That's very like what we ask of a poet.'

'Should we call that truth, though? Shouldn't we rather call it "convincingness" or something?'

'Call it what you like. It's still the same.'

'Then there's consistency. Philosophers have to be consistent, but a poet can contradict himself and no one cares: very well, he contradicts himself.'

'Consistency is a lot more than not contradicting yourself, surely. It means that the sum of what you say must hang together, you must make out a good case in general.'

'Quite. And poets don't have to make out cases.'

'No, but there's something they do have to do that's rather like it. Their poems have to have a sort of unity, be all of the same consistency if you like. Imagery has to be "in keeping," transitions must be graceful and movements easy, and a formal balance must be kept up over all. I'm not sure this isn't the same demand we make on philosophy, the demand that the thing should "come off." '

'I don't agree with you at all. And if I did, what about cogency? Poems don't have to be well argued. But the most important of all the demands we make of philosophy is surely that its proofs must be valid and its reasons sound.'

Francis thought for a moment. I was afraid he was going to say something about 'reasons of the heart,' but even he stopped short of that. 'All right,' he said at last. 'Truth, consistency and convincingness are common or have analogues, but cogency isn't and, so far as I can see, doesn't. One out of four. Next candidate, please.'

'How about significance? You said yourself that the meaninglessness philosophers complain of in other philosophers is a purely logical defect. Poets don't need to be logical. I should think you could put significance alongside cogency as a standard for philosophy but not for poetry.'

'Yes, I did say that. But it's a funny thing about meaninglessness. The cry goes up before the criterion is applied. Suppose a canon of verifiability or what not fails to condemn what the critic dislikes. He doesn't decide that the attack was misdirected, he decides that the criterion was wrongly formulated.'

'So?'

'So the cry of "meaningless!" must really express a sort of aesthetic distaste that is subsequently rationalized. If the objection were really logical, the formulation of the criterion would determine what was acceptable.'

'I still don't see any application to poetry.'

'Well, no, not really, but there are analogous distastes, though they are more various and even vaguer. Imagery mustn't be too esoteric, for one thing.'

'Where's the analogy?'

'In the demand that what is said must be open to confirmation in public experience. Only instead of verified fact there is shared experience.'

'It isn't merely distaste, then, it really is a sort of logical demand.'

'Oh, am I proving too much? Sorry.'

'That's quite all right. What are the other various demands?'

'I can't remember, you shouldn't have interrupted.'

'I'm sorry.'

'That's quite all right. Oh yes, I know, poetic diction mustn't be trite, it must be faithful to the quality of the experience it refers to. That's all I can think of just now.'

'That's that fidelity you were talking about before. You can't put it in twice.'

'I was thinking of it more as a demand for propriety of language this time. You know, something has to get said.'

'The analogy's pretty feeble, anyway. Still, if it's the best you can do. . . .'

'I'm going to claim it all the same, on the strength of the esoteric imagery bit. One out of five. Next candidate, please.'

Actually I had more to offer, but before this could become apparent the secretary stepped in. 'Seriousness,' he said. 'I feel strongly, and many others feel with me, that a philosopher should devote himself to the serious concerns of mankind, whereas you and your friends do nothing but quibble about technical trifles.'

'That's a little unfair,' I said. 'You don't make any such demand of any other discipline. I should have thought the condition of progress in any science was a tolerance of waste of time. Unless you're ready to give endless pains to lines of enquiry that may lead nowhere you can't hope to break through anywhere unforeseen. I don't see that you have any call to complain of our going into questions that don't seem important to you, so long as someone is tackling your big and obvious questions for you. And surely someone always is.'

'But their work is of such poor quality. All the most competent and scrupulous men fritter their lives away on trivia.'

'Has it ever occurred to you, that if you think all the brightest people are doing the wrong thing, and only the numbskulls are doing the right thing, there may be something amiss with your scale of values? What you prize is what the numbskulls prize.'

'That isn't very kind,' said Francis. 'The poor man has a point, surely. It isn't too hard to deal thoroughly with small issues, so that's what most people do. But it takes for ever to deal thoroughly with big issues, and that's why no one does it. The best you can do is to pick out the key questions and the key points to them, but that's tremendously hard and scarcely anyone can do even that. On the other hand, it's obviously no use at all doing a sloppy job on a trivial question, so all the sloppiest-minded people pick out the biggest topics. It's all perfectly natural, but no wonder people complain.'

'And what about poetry?' asked Kitty.

'Same thing, very nearly. The most competent poetry nowadays is sensitive and subtle, but interesting only to people interested in poetry. Fair enough, why should anyone else care? But people would like to feel that poets were saying something worth taking seriously about their everyday concerns or their Sunday aspirations. But as it is, if you want anything more than Mr Larkin's doubts about whether to wear cycle clips in church, what have you got? Nothing but A. dreadful Noyes.'

'My husband often makes jokes,' Kitty explained.

'Seriously, people want us to be a lot of Shakespeares, and it would be nice if we were but it isn't reasonable to ask it.'

'Your analogy appears to me to be exact at all points,' said the secretary, 'alike in the demands made on poets and philosophers and in the reasons for disappointment. I congratulate you.'

'Thank you. One out of six. Next.'

'You *cryptic* boy,' said Xanthippe. 'One out of six what? It's *marvellous* to have you keeping score, it makes us feel so *secure*, but we would like to know what we're playing, especially as you seem to be winning all the time. I mean, it's *lovely* for you to make up the rules and keep the score, and we don't mind losing, but *do* tell us what we're losing *at*.'

'Six criteria of excellence, one peculiar to philosophy, five shared.'

'Distance!' said Xanthippe.

'Eh?'

'The lady said "distance,"' said Kitty. 'You know, the stuff that lends enchantment to views.'

'That's what I thought she said. What am I supposed to do? Stand up and cheer?'

'The *rudeness* of the man! I'll have you know that in *my* young days, if you can imagine such a thing, *all* the best critics said *all* the best poets went around being detached and ironical and *mature*.'

'They said that, did they?'

'My dears, you should have *heard* them. And isn't that *just* like you philosophers? Impartiality isn't the *half* of it. You're all so far above the battle I'd like to shoot you down in *flames*.'

'That's certainly the required pose. One out of seven.'

'Don't you think this irony business is a bit overdone?' I said. 'If the attitude comes naturally to a poet, fine, but if it's deliberately assumed I find it tiresome in the extreme.'

'How do you know when it's assumed?' said Socrates.

'I don't really. I should have said, when it seems to be deliberately adopted.'

'I quite agree,' said Francis; 'and I think the same is true in philosophy. When a philosopher is really disinterested, like you, Socrates, that's magnificent. But usually the air of impartiality is assumed to cover up some log-rolling or skulduggery, and then I think it's just disgusting.'

'But how do you know—?' began Socrates.

'Oh, *never mind* how!' shouted Francis. 'I'm sorry, Socrates, but really you do take all the fun out of a conversation.'

'Some fun is better removed,' said Socrates, calmly.

'*Squabble*, squabble,' said Xanthippe. 'Siggy doesn't mean to be annoying, it's the way he's made, isn't it, dear? Now you just listen to me while I even the score up. I've been reading *another* good book, by a Professor of *Latin* if you can believe me, and it tells you *all* about how to tell good poetry, if you're a man. You lather your face, you see, and start shaving, and then you start reciting the poetry, and if you cut yourself it's *good*.⁶ Of course we poor little girls don't shave, so we can't do it. I suppose that's why women don't make good critics, *poor us. Two* out of seven.'

'Eight.'

'How *lovely* to be clever and *right* all the time. *Anyway*, philosophy doesn't have to be thrilling, that I *do* know.'

'That's what *you* think,' said Francis nastily. 'People are always complaining about aesthetics for being boring and dreary. Why should they complain, if it isn't meant to be thrilling and gay?'

'*I* think they're just being silly!'

'So is your chum with the shaving brush.'

'But he was a *Professor*, dear. Of *Latin*.'

'The people who complain about aesthetics being dull are professors of philosophy. *One* out of eight.'

'Oh, all *right*, you're *mean*.'

'I feel,' said the secretary, 'that Xanthippe would have done better to claim as a specific excellence of poetry its quasi-musical properties. Surely rhyme, rhythm, and euphony generally are of prime importance in verse; but I can think of nothing comparable in the evaluation of philosophy.'

'Philosophy should be well written,' I said.

'No doubt. But stylistic faults are not philosophical demerits, provided that they do not obscure the argument.'

'Some philosophers write badly on purpose,' said Francis, 'so as not to be taken for amateurs. Two out of nine.'

'Then again,' said the secretary, 'poetry is expected to be polysemous.'

'You made that word up.'

'I did not. It is a technical term of semantics. It denotes a certain semantic richness. A poet like Shakespeare can be enjoyed on more than one level—'

'Stalls, circle, and gallery,' said Kitty.

'Ha ha. Most amusing. The best poetry, as I was saying, possesses a significance beyond the literal. It suggests more than it states. It abounds in ambiguities, of which I believe scholars have identified no less than seven varieties.[7] Whereas, surely, a philosopher should mean one thing only, and any overtones that his words may have are merely irritating.'

'True for you,' said Francis. 'Three out of ten. Any more?'

'He should mean no more than he says, because he should say no less than he means,' pursued the secretary, who saw no reason to waste a good epigram just because the subject was closed.

'All right, we got the point. No one got anything else to suggest?'

Apparently no one did; or, if they had, they were unwilling to encourage Francis any further in his somewhat egotistic performance.

'All right, then. I take it, with seven points of likeness and only three of difference, we are prepared to concede that poetry and philosophy are more alike than they are different?'

'Don't be absurd,' I said. 'It's three horses to seven rabbits. It's no good losing sight of the fact that poetry and philosophy just are quite different. The basic intentions are altogether unlike. Everything else is incidental. And then of course there's the institutional background. I mean, poets and philosophers have different jobs, move in different circles, are paid differently, publish in different media, think of themselves differently.'

'I suppose you're right. But at least I've shown that they do have a lot in common, much more than you'd expect.'

'Perhaps we might grant you this much,' said the secretary, 'that philosophy and poetry are to be grouped together with other humane studies in opposition to the natural sciences. The latter seek definite solutions to definite problems in accordance with definite rules, whereas the former admit of much more freedom of approach. One might say that this liberty of manoeuvre makes of philosophy a branch of literature rather than a science. Similarly, poet and philosopher seem by the nature of their undertaking to be personally committed in their work in a way in which the scientific worker is not.'

'I think that's just an illusion,' said Francis. 'Your phrase "scientific worker" gives you away. You're contrasting different levels of creativity, not different disciplines. What's confused you is that the stereotype of the scientist has fastened on the level of routine plodding, but the stereotype of the philosopher has fastened on the level of original thought. What you ought to contrast is the methodical scientific investigator with the methodical literary hack and the plodding philosophical thesis-monger; or the scientific trailblazer with the literary or philosophical genius. After all, we did distinguish two kinds of writing in poetry and philosophy alike, and I'm sure the same sort of duality applies to what scientists do. Original work in science doesn't come from method and routine alone, you know. It depends on developing new ways of looking at things and doing things. And I never heard that fresh ideas flowed any more steadily there than anywhere else, or that ways of discovering could be more consciously controlled.'

'Are you trying to tell us,' I said, 'that science is no more scientific than the humanities? Scientists can't go around being inspirational. What about experimental method? What about all the mathematics?'

'Well, what about them? Of course the sciences have their own techniques. So does poetry, so does anything. Techniques separate disciplines, it's the uncertainties of invention that unite them. And is there really any set of techniques that is peculiar to science as such? I think there are just sciences, each with its own technique. Of course the techniques overlap, but they overlap with other pursuits too. I've never met a scientist: they're all chemists, or physicists, or botanists, or something. People think it's all one thing because the same poor clunk has to teach them all at school. You might as well think that poetry was a kind of football because the games master taught English. If you lined up the contrasts that really matter, experiment against mathematics, discovery against interpretation and so on, I don't think you'd find the sciences all on one side of any of them. When I think of science I don't think of a mysterious indivisible intellectual monster, I think of a lot of people doing the best they can.'

'I really do not have the special knowledge to say whether or not you are right,' said the secretary, 'but I must say that I suspect you of exaggeration, inaccuracy and special pleading.'

'Don't worry,' said Kitty, 'Francis doesn't know a thing about science, he just likes to feel he has a foot in each culture.'

'Perhaps I can disentangle one solid proposition from the verbiage. You began by saying that the "creative process" was no less common among philosophers than among poets. Now you are maintaining that it is associated with original thought in any field, even among the exact sciences. Am I right?'

'Absolutely. Any original thinker, doesn't matter what he does, depends on being able to keep coming up with good fresh ideas. And there's just nothing he can do about it. When the novel solution comes it just comes. How it's related to its problem-stimulus is something he simply doesn't know. He can't explain how he does it, even to himself. He just has to hope that new ideas will keep turning up. But whatever it is, it's this knack of repeated success, with all the stresses and anxieties and ferments that go with it, that makes up what you call the "creative process."'

'Have you finished, Francis?' said Kitty. 'Because it's time we got home and gave the kids their food, and you can't talk while you're punting.'

'My dear, he *does!*' said Xanthippe. 'That's what's so *awful.*'

'I've hardly started. This unreliability of invention is only a special case of something that holds quite generally: the mind can't command the success of its own operations. Stammerers never know in advance whether they'll be able to bring out a particular word. Sometimes I can raise one eyebrow without the other like this— there! but sometimes I can't, and I never know in advance whether I shall be able to "find" the appropriate muscle. If I can't, there's no method of searching for it that I can rely on. It's the same with a writer. He hopes he'll come up with something, but there's no way of making sure.'

'Well, of course not,' I said. 'As Socrates was saying, you can't be sure you have the answer to a problem till you have it.'

'No, but if there's a method you can be fairly sure you *will* get it. All you have to do is follow the procedure. It's when you get beyond methods that you have real uncertainty and anxiety.'

'Aren't we being a bit neurotic about this?'

'Not at all. There really is something to worry about. Of course, you aren't likely to contract a hysterical paralysis and be unable to lift your arm when you want to, and you're not likely to develop a stammer at your age. You might of course, but it's not worth bothering over. But intellectuals do often find the day come when their gift fails them. They run out of ideas. How many poets, philosophers, mathematicians, go on being creative all their lives? Not many. Why do you suppose they stop? They just don't have any ideas any more. The oracles are silent. There isn't a thing they can do about it. And who wants to be an extinct volcano?'

'Me, please,' said Xanthippe. 'Bags Cotopaxi, or hasn't it gone out yet?'

'Oh, shut up.'

'Well,' said Socrates, 'I don't expect ever to run out of questions to ask. Come to think of it, it's always the same question, though it seems just as good as ever. But it's perfectly true I don't feel like asking it quite so often as I did.'

'I have often heard it said,' said the secretary, 'that poets are not truly the authors of their poems, but rather the people in whom the poems happen. And it is also said that one should never say "I think," but rather "It thinks in me."'

'*Clever* it!' said Xanthippe. 'Who is it?'

'I take it that the impersonal form has the same function as the passive voice. No doubt the saying is rendered from the German or some such tongue. I cite these locutions merely as testifying to an attitude similar to that which the professor has avouched.'

'Some of our colleagues,' I said, 'have thought of the intellect as an impersonal somewhat in which men might share, rather than as something of a man's own.[8] I wonder if that was because people can't predict and control what their minds will do.'

'Surely that was rather because intellectual abstractions are unrelated in their content to the personal life histories of this man or that.'

'Yes, I suppose it was. But one might be led to say the same thing by reflecting that one can hardly claim authorship where control is so uncertain.'

'Possibly,' said Francis, 'but you're still assuming that the uncertainty is peculiar to the intellectual life. I've told you that it isn't really. It's just that the risk of failure in intellectual affairs is more of a live possibility for most of us. Actually, our decisions to do things are no more neccessarily effective even within our bodies than our decisions to have a new idea or to solve a problem would be. They just work more often. All our words for activities are "achievement verbs" in this way. In the physical realm, the rare failures point up the almost unvarying success. I know it's not fashionable to say these things, but aren't they true? And isn't it important not to forget them? Both as thinker and as agent, a man is a mystery to himself. I think philosophy should come to terms with this mystery, either by accommodating it or dispelling it.'

'Oh, what a *lovely* thought!' said Xanthippe. '"Man is a mystery to himself." I'm sure that's *profoundly* true. It makes me feel like saying "Yea, *verily*."'

'You don't have to, because it isn't what I said. "Man" doesn't have a self to be a mystery to. I said *a* man, *each* man, is a mystery to himself. In the sense, I mean, that he really hasn't the faintest idea how he keeps on going as a conscious being. It's no good describing the physiological machinery, because you can't get at it. It's no good telling a paralytic that if he could get an electric discharge down some nerve or other he could flex this or that muscle and that would move his leg for him. He can *try* moving his leg, though it won't do any good. He can't even try to operate his nervous system.'

'I wonder,' said the secretary, diffidently. We looked at him in astonishment. He blushed. 'It just occurred to me,' he went on, 'that one might do something towards dispelling the mystery you were talking about by considering the terms in which we speak of action and thought. There's such a likeness, isn't there, between first-person and third-person forms. I mean, we use the same words for what we do and for what other people do. But really, nothing we do seems at the time in the least like anything other people do. "I'm running" sounds very like "he's running," but really what I know of my running is totally unlike what I know of anyone else's running. My running is all effort and panting and pounding, and slowly changing perspectives all round. Anyone else's running is a figure floating through a still landscape. Part of the difference is that we feel ourselves making ourselves run, if you see what I mean, but we see other people just running. Am I making myself clear?'

The secretary's tentative manner, so unlike his usual one and so reminiscent of his younger days, staggered us all so much that it was a second or two before any of us could answer. 'Perfectly clear,' I said, 'so far.'

'Well, what I'm getting at is this. People often talk as if we start by knowing all about ourselves and then find out about other people, so that there could be a real problem about whether other people are real, whether they aren't just dream-figures of one's own, or automata at best. So people come to think that solipsism might be a possible position.'

'All clear so far,' I said, as encouragingly as I could, for the poor man was twisting his fingers and looking shy—a grotesque spectacle, as you may suppose.

'Well, the thing is, you see, there aren't any solipsists. Now, why aren't there? I think it's because the way we usually talk about things people do doesn't take any account of the way they seem to people doing them, but only of how they seem to others. We talk about ourselves as if we were other people, unless we are being confessional. And of course this is the natural way to talk, because we mostly talk to other people, and to other people *we* are other people. So the whole structure of our thought and language is built up on the third-person model. So the real problem isn't whether other people are real like ourselves, but whether we are real like other people. I wonder if the reason why we are mysteries to ourselves isn't just that the third-person view implied in the structure of our thought doesn't fit the first-person view we have of ourselves. What the mystery comes down to is this: why can't I find in myself anything corresponding to the wholeness and simplicity implied in a spectator's account of another's actions? And of course the answer is perfectly simple, it's because I am an agent and not a spectator. I think that solves what for me is the real mystery, though the professor didn't mention it, and that is, *why* a man should be mysterious to himself when he's never known anything different. The answer is that he is led by the structure of thought and language to slight this knowledge. To dispel the mystery the professor spoke of, one would have to construct some account of the concepts of thought and action that would take first-person views as seriously as third-person ones. Or am I on the wrong track altogether?'

'No, I don't think so,' I said. 'I don't think you could ever explain away the anxiety that a man who lives by his wits is bound to feel when he considers that his wits are going to get rusty some day. You might get the mysteriousness out of the mystery, though. That would be something.'

'Tell us,' said Francis, 'did you think of all that yourself?'

'Well,' said the secretary, 'a lot of it is common property, of course, but I don't remember finding anything in the literature exactly like what I said.'

'Good lord!' said Francis. 'You don't mean to tell us you're going to set up as a philosopher on your own account, after all these years?'

'Well, you know,' said the secretary, 'perhaps I might. I really think perhaps I might.'

'And now,' said Xanthippe, 'we *must* get home to supper, or the children will be *casting lots* for whom to eat first. *Do* come and join us, Xenny dear, I can *easily* pop another carrot in the pot for you.'

But I declined, and they all got into their punt and pushed off downstream into the shadow of the trees, the secretary poling them at high speed with all his usual air of determination and capacity. I have not seen any of them since.[9] When I followed on an hour later after eating my own sandwiches the river was deserted and the boat-house already closed. By the time I had pitched my little tent on the dew-soaked grass of Port Meadow the night had turned clear and cold. As I unrolled my sleeping-bag I thought: my friends are right, I am getting too old for this sort of thing.

Ferris Wheel

Look for me if you love me
I'll not be there
not in the Hall of Mirrors
not anywhere
but in my element
the shrieking air ...

Notes

INTRODUCTION AND WARNING

1. Friedrich Nietzsche, *Werke* (Leipzig, 1923), 14, 353-54.

FRANCISCUS

1. Those unfamiliar with Socrates' methods in arithmetic may appreciate a little help in working out this date. The first good number is 3; it is made flat by squaring (9) and solid by cubing (27). Applied three times, this makes $3 \times 27 = 81$ generations from Socrates' birth in 469 B.C. If Socrates reckons 30 years to a generation, 81 generations are 2430 years, which brings us, I fear, to 1962. If Socrates is reckoning three generations to a century we have a few years in hand (A.D. 2232).

2. In case you have not been keeping score, the eight types of riddle these young people have distinguished are (1) concealed description, (2) punning conundrums, (3) nonsensical pseudoconundrums with irrelevant 'answers,' (4) seeming conundrums with irregular answers, (5) conundrums meant to exploit the admission of ignorance, (6) dilemmas meant to embarrass the solver, (7) ambiguous riddles in which the poser chooses whichever interpretation the solver neglects, and (8) riddles whose answer is a concealed description of what the riddle names. If I ever see Francis again, I must ask him what he would have said about the 'elephant jokes' that became popular about twenty years after this conversation took place. Fundamentally, the 'elephant joke' was no more than a riddle or series of riddles one or more of which referred to an elephant either in question or answer. But most of them were parasitic forms. There had already existed parasitic riddles of a kind that Francis left out, those in which new answers were found for old conundrums: for example, in the traditional conundrum 'What's black and white and red all over?', 'A sun-burned zebra' was substituted for the traditional 'A newspaper.' Some elephant jokes were similar variants on established riddles: for example, that just quoted underlies the following: 'What's red and white on the outside and grey on the inside?'—'Campbell's cream of

elephant soup.' But the most characteristic parasites were preceded by their own hosts: 'Why do ducks have webbed feet?'—'To stamp out forest fires'— 'Why do elephants have broad feet?'—'To stamp out flaming ducks.' Some sequences were elaborate: 'What's the difference between an elephant and a plum?'—'Elephants are grey, plums are purple'—'What did Tarzan say when he saw a herd of elephants coming over the hill?'—'Here's a herd of elephants coming over the hill'—'What did Tarzan say when he saw the same herd of elephants coming over the hill, wearing sunglasses?'—'Nothing, he didn't recognize them'—'What did Jane say when she saw a herd of purple elephants coming over the hill '—'Here come the plums.' I suspect that Francis would have found here nothing more than a confirmation of his thesis about ritual form and its compulsive effect.

3. Maurice must mean N. R. Campbell, who says on page 164 of his *Physics: the Elements* (Cambridge, 1920): 'Observations do not become part of science until they are ordered, and this ordering involves the discovery of laws; any observations which have not been, to some extent, ordered in laws do not form part of science.' Campbell's remarks about experiments, to which the secretary refers later, may be found on page 112 of the same book.

4. Professor John Wisdom says this on page 428 of *The Philosophy of G. E. Moore*, ed. P. A. Schilpp (Evanston, 1942).

5. This is a delicate compliment to Socrates, being a quotation from Plato's *Theaetetus*, 167a.

IS REALITY REALLY REAL?

1. F. H. Bradley, *Appearance and Reality* (London, 1893), xiv. But it would be a pity if his words were taken to justify those 'psychoanalytical' explainings-away of philosophy that seek bad instincts for what men believe upon reasons.

2. G. E. Moore, *Philosophical Studies* (London, 1922), ch. 6.

3. Morris Lazerowitz, 'Moore's Paradox,' in *The Philosophy of G. E. Moore*, ed. P. A. Schilpp (Evanston: 1942), pp. 369-93.

4. *Principles of Logic* (London, 1922), p. 188.

5. For example, Sir David Ross in his edition of Aristotle's *Physics* (Oxford, 1936), pp. 71-85.

6. G. R. G. Mure, *Introduction to Hegel* (Oxford: 1940), p. 3. He also says (*ibid.*) that 'real' can only mean 'the opposite of the sham'—a point that, as we have remarked, Austin makes too.

7. See my *Enquiry into Goodness* (Toronto: 1958), §6.1632.

8. Cf. J. L. Austin, *Sense and Sensibilia* (Oxford, 1962), ch. 7.

9. These theses were derived from the late Professor Austin's lectures, a later version of which appears in the work mentioned in note 8. This portion of the lectures underwent considerable change in the course of the years (cf. Mr. Warnock's Foreword, pp. v-vii); my notes represent the version of 1949, no doubt inaccurately. It is immaterial whether these theses can justly be attributed to Austin: my argument requires them in this form, whatever their source.

10. This suggestion is derived from a series of lectures on Berkeley delivered by Sir Isaiah Berlin at Oxford University in the Hilary term, 1950. As with Austin's lectures, the form and context of the original utterance may not be that of my use of it, the latter being determined by the needs of the present argument.

11. *Philosophical Studies*, p. 199.

12. Martin Heidegger, *Being and Time* (New York, 1962), pp. 91-148.

13. *The Meaning of Truth* (New York, 1909), p. 132.
14. S. E. Toulmin, *The Place of Reason in Ethics* (Cambridge, 1950), ch. 8.
15. *Philosophical Studies*, p. 3.
16. *Some Problems of Philosophy* (New York, 1911), p. 101.
17. Hans Reichenbach, *Elements of Symbolic Logic* (New York, 1947), p. 348.
18. Gabriel Marcel, *The Philosophy of Existence* (London, 1948), p. 85.

THE CENTRAL PROBLEM OF PHILOSOPHY

1. By John H. Mueller in the *American Journal of Sociology*, 51 (1945-6): 276-82. The remarks in the text, though not untrue, are unjust to an article whose intention was purely methodological. The injustice may be put down to the excited frame of mind that the sequel sufficiently attests.
2. By an 'experience' I mean here something that happens to a person as it seems to him when it happens—that is, a happening as seen 'from the inside' and not by a third party.
3. Clive Bell, *Art* (London, 1914). For a less indulgent interpretation of Mr. Bell, see H. Osborne, *Theory of Beauty* (London, 1952), p. 68.
4. *The Elementary Forms of the Religious Life* (London, 1915). Further remarks on this analogy may be found in my *Structure of Aesthetics* (Toronto, 1963), pp. 24-25, 295-96.
5. This and other citations of Professor Lewis refer to the essay 'On Poetic Truth' in his *Morals and Revelation* (London, 1951), pp. 232-55.
6. H. H. Farmer, *Revelation and Religion* (London, 1954), ch. 1. Someone has said that 'There are only two ways of making a man a Christian: by conversion, and by definition.'
7. See W. W. Jaeger, *Aristotle* (Oxford, 1948), 106ff.; texts in *Aristotelis Fragmenta Selecta* (Oxford, 1955), Carmina 2 and 4.
8. Thomas Aquinas, *Summa Theologiae*, Ia IIae, q.63, and Q. *Disp. de Virtute*, q.1 a.10; Augustine, *The City of God*, V, 12ff.
9. Cf. Martin Buber, *I and Thou* (Edinburgh, 1937), 7ff.
10. Nietzsche, *Werke*, ed. K. von Schlechta, Vol. 3 (Munich, 1956), 680.
11. Cf. M. Untersteiner's discussion of Protagoras in *The Sophists* (New York, 1954).
12. N. R. Campbell, *Physics: the Elements* (Cambridge: 1920), p. 132.

INTERLUDE

1. E. L. Fackenheim, *Metaphysics and Historicity* (Milwaukee, 1961).

SPECULATION AND REFLECTION

1. Parmenides, fragment B3 (Diels-Kranz, 6th edition).
2. S. Kierkegaard, *Fear and Trembling* and *The Sickness Unto Death* (New York, 1954), p. 177.
3. Democritus, fragment B165 (Diels-Kranz, 6th edition).
4. There is admittedly a loose sense of 'definition' in which the *Iliad* might be said to be the definition of 'The *Iliad*'. One might therefore suppose that a complete collection of exhaustive biographies would be the definition of 'man.' But this is not so: reasons were given in 'Is Reality Really Real?' for

thinking that no narrative, however long, can embrace the whole of any experience.

5. Karl Jaspers, *Reason and Existenz* (New York, 1955), p. 26.

6. Dio Chrysostom, *Orationes*, LXX, 8.

7. Walter Kaufmann, ed., *Existentialism from Dostoevsky to Sartre* (New York, 1956), pp. 290-91.

8. René Descartes, *Discourse on Method*, Part 2. In his *Philosophical Works*, trans. Haldane and Ross (Cambridge: 1931), I: 87.

9. Edward Caird, *Essays on Literature and Philosophy* (Glasgow, 1892), p. 268.

10. David Hume, *A Treatise on Human Nature*, ed. L. A. Selby-Bigge (Oxford, 1888), p. 269.

11. James Boswell, *The Life of Samuel Johnson, LL.D.*, Everyman edition (London, 1949), I: 292.

12. *A Treatise on Human Nature*, p. 253.

13. Walter Pater, *The Renaissance*, 5th ed. (London: 1912), pp. 234-35.

14. George Berkeley, 'Third Dialogue,' in his *New Theory of Vision* etc., Everyman edition (London: 1910), pp. 274-75.

15. Plato, *Philebus*, 28c.

16. Extinct, that is, except among theologians, who after prying the *kerygma* loose from a mummified mythology are trying to shackle it to this fresher corpse.

17. Friedrich Nietzsche, *Beyond Good and Evil* (Chicago: 1955), p. 186.

18. R. M. Hare, 'A School for Philosophers,' *Ratio* 2 (1959-60): 107-20.

19. Leo Tolstoy, *What Is Art?*, in *Tolstoy on Art* (London: 1924), p. 224.

20. Cf. Plato, *Republic*, 588b ff.

21. I have developed this theme further in 'The Concept of Purpose', *Ethics* 72 (1962): 157-70.

22. Karl Jaspers, *Way to Wisdom* (New Haven: 1954), pp. 12-14, 121-22, and *passim*.

23. Cf. Aristotle, *Metaphysics*, IV, 5.

24. Cf. E. H. Gombrich, *Art and Illusion* (New York: 1960).

25. Plato, *Euthydemus*, 283d-285c.

INTERLUDE

1. Marshall McLuhan, *Understanding Media* (New York: 1964), ch. 2.

2. S. T. Coleridge, *Shakespearean Criticism*, ed. T. M. Raysor (London: 1960), I: 114-16, 176-80.

3. R. G. Collingwood, *Essay on Philosophical Method* (Oxford: 1933), pp. 213-14.

XANTHIPPE

1. I was thinking of *The Road to Xanadu*, by John Livingston Lowes (Boston: 1927). Kitty presumably had in mind Professor Graves' remarks in *The Crowning Privilege* (Harmondsworth: 1959), p. 214.

2. Actually, I don't think it does. But she does say, in *Feeling and Form* (London: 1953), p. 252: 'Poetry is not genuine discourse at all, but is the creating of an illusory "experience," or a piece of virtual history, by means of discursive language, . . .'

3. He maintains it in the Fifth Article of *Beyond Good and Evil*, where he says (§187) that moralities are a 'symbolic language of the passions.'

4. After speaking of 'sub-conscious incubation,' Russell writes in *Portraits from Memory* (London: 1956), p. 195: 'Suddenly, the solution emerged with blinding clarity, so that it only remained to write down what had appeared as if in a revelation.' There is a stage-army of similar testimonies from scientists, paraded most availably by Professor W. I. B. Beveridge in *The Art of Scientific Investigation* (New York: 1950).

5. Francis is probably referring to Wang Yü's *Tung-chuan Lun Hua*, which he quotes in his *Structure of Aesthetics* (Toronto: 1963), p. 414. Kitty may be thinking of what Professor Graves says on and around page 124 of *The Crowning Privilege*.

6. Xanthippe is obviously alluding to A. E. Housman, *The Name and Nature of Poetry* (Cambridge: 1933).

7. This is not perhaps a very happy description of what William Empson did in *Seven Types of Ambiguity* (London: 1930).

8. This idea is adumbrated in Aristotle's *Nicomachean Ethics*, X, 7, and *De Anima*, III, 5, and is formally developed and elaborated in the system of Plotinus.

9. I forgot to ask Francis about those elephants.